॥ श्रीः ॥

॥ स्वात्मनिरूपणम् ॥

Svātmanirūpanam

The True Definition of One's Own Self

॥ श्रीः ॥

॥ स्वात्मनिरूपणम् ॥

Svātmanirūpanam

sva	**one's/one's own**
ātma	**Self**
nirūpaṇam	**definition**
	or
su	**good/well/excellent/true**
ātma	**Self**
nirūpaṇam	**definition**

Definition of one's own Self
The good definition of the Self
Definition of the good Self
Definition of the true Self
The true definition of the Self

Translation by
Dr. H. Ramamoorthy
&
Nome

Society of Abidance in Truth

First Edition 2002
Second Edition 2023

For Sale Outside USA

ISBN 978-1-947154-26-1

FOR ALL INQUIRIES, CONTACT THE PUBLISHER:
Society of Abidance in Truth
SAT
1834 Ocean Street
Santa Cruz, California 95060 USA
(831) 425-7287
sat@satramana.org
www.SATRamana.org

Foreword

Om Namo Bhagavate Sri Sankaraya
Om Namo Bhagavate Sri Ramanaya

It is a great blessing for the Society of Abidance in Truth (SAT) to be able to present this work by Sri Sankara.

SAT's fundamental purpose is to bring forth the universal, perennial wisdom of Advaita Vedanta in a profound, experiential manner as has been handed down by great sages such as Sri Sankara and Sri Ramana Maharshi. We are extraordinarily grateful to those spiritual beings from antiquity who recorded these precious, life-fulfilling teachings for all serious spiritual seekers to meditate deeply upon with the wise guidance of a Sat-Guru in order to unlock their meaning, understand the true significance of life, and realize at heart the pure essence of these sacred texts.

The scripture presented here, composed by the glorious Sat-Guru Sri Sankara, has been translated from Sanskrit into English by Dr. H. Ramamoorthy and Nome to serve a meditative purpose and, thus, remove unreal bondage. It is sincerely hoped by the translators and SAT that nothing has been left out or has been modified in any manner and that this translation retains the pristine teaching as Sri Sankara intended.

Each verse has been presented in four versions. The first is the original Sanskrit; the second is the romanized version which can be used for recitation purposes by those who do not read Sanskrit; the third is a word-for-word breakdown; and the fourth is a running translation in fluent English. The purpose of the four versions is to provide a thorough presentation for spiritual beings, regardless of their language abilities, so that all have the opportunity to understand the teaching as presented by Sri Sankara.

SAT is also grateful to have had the privilege of producing other such works by Sri Sankara such as *Nirguna Manasa Puja* and by the great sage Ribhu such as *The Ribhu Gita* (English translation from Sanskrit) and *The Song of Ribhu* (English translation from Tamil). Numerous Advaita Vedanta texts and stotra-s (hymns) composed by Sri Sankara, writings of Sri Ramana Maharshi, and Upanishad and Agama texts, translated by the same translation team, are also planned for future publication.

These sacred writings are beacons of Reality appearing in a dream. If this work serves to free but a single being from the illusory clutches of samsara, it has fulfilled its divine purpose.

Sasvati

Guru Purnima, July 24, 2002

Acknowledgements

The translators and the Society of Abidance in Truth would like to express their deepest gratitude to:

Ganesh Sadasivan, Raman Muthukrishnan and Sangeeta Raman for their careful proofreading of this text.

S. Venkataramanan whose Sanskrit text and English translation, published by G.A. Natesan and Co., Madras, over sixty-five years ago, helped clarify a few points and provided an alternative Sanskrit edition of Sankara's words for certain verses.

All the members of SAT who, through their dedicated efforts and offerings, enable SAT to continue in its consecrated endeavor to make these timeless teachings of nondualistic Self-Knowledge available to earnest seekers of Truth.

Sasvati for her typing and layout of this book, seeing to its printing, and helping to provide an environment that was conducive to the translators' concentrated work.

All the sages, both those whom we know by name and those whom we do not, who have revealed and preserved this Supreme Knowledge and who have been the inspiration of the present work.

Introduction

Being is. Being alone is. The Self is the Absolute, and That is the only Reality. Such is eternally the Truth. Such is the final conclusion of Advaita Vedanta.

This *Svatmanirupanam (Definition of One's Own Self)*, authored by the great sage of Advaita Vedanta, Adi Sankara, is a concise text of this enlightening teaching. As the title declares, it is the teaching regarding the true definition of the Self. The Self is itself Brahman, the vast, formless Absolute, and any contrariwise conception of it is merely delusion. So, this teaching is an exposition of what is truly the Self. As there are not actually two selves, for the true Self is the ever-existent and a false self is never-existent, and since one being the object of another is impossible, this teaching is of the nature of one's own Self. The teaching is the revelation of the Self for the purpose of Self-Realization for those who earnestly inquire to know within themselves the answer to the question, "Who am I?"

The nondualistic teachings expressed here by Sri Sankaracharya, the great spiritual teacher Sankara, are of an eternal nature. This is so not only because of the timeless meaning or content of these teachings, dealing as they do with the Self that transcends all time, space, and objectivized illusion, but also because they form the very core and the original quintessence of Advaita Vedanta, which is the final, highest Knowledge. Advaita Vedanta is itself the very essence of Sanatana Dharma,[1] the teachings of eternal Truth. The very same teachings are found in the *Upanisad-s*, which are the wisdom portion of the *Veda-s*, which are perhaps the most ancient extant scriptures. These very same teachings of Self-Realization and of the Self-inquiry that results in this

---

[1] *Also referred to as Hinduism.*

Realization have been taught more recently with superlative clarity by Bhagavan Sri Ramana Maharshi. Indeed, the pure emphasis on the Knowledge of one's own Self found in this *Svatmanirupanam* is extremely reminiscent of the teachings given so graciously by the Maharshi, teachings which, when comprehended and thoroughly practiced, unfailingly yield Liberation from all of the imagined bondage. The resultant silent peace and illimitable bliss, of the very nature of the Being-Consciousness that is the Self, are ineffable. It is wondrous that, though transcendent of words and thoughts, the Truth is so clearly revealed by the great sages. The records of their teachings are veritable, inextinguishable lights that have been preserved and handed down for ages. Those who are graced to receive such are blessed, indeed.

These teachings of the *Svatmanirupanam*, which are intended to bring Liberation from the bondage of ignorance, are of Self-Knowledge. This Knowledge is that of Consciousness itself by Consciousness itself. Consciousness is identical with Being, so this Knowledge is that of Being itself. It is something utterly non-bodily and non-sensory in nature. It is also non-mental in nature. Knowledge through the senses or through thoughts may be regarded as indirect or as just of the nature of ignorance. Such ignorant "knowledge" is based on the erroneous notions of an "I" to be a knower or experiencer, a "this" or an existent objective thing, and the relation between them. Such dualism or triadic notions are characteristic of ignorance. True Knowledge is characterized by nonduality. In true Knowledge, there remains no notion of individuality, or an ego, no matter what attributes may be further superimposed on that notion, such as a thinker, a sensing entity, an embodied entity, and so forth and so on. In True Knowledge, there remains no notion of a "this," whether such a world or realm of objectivized experiences or notions be conceived of as permanent or temporary, as of matter or of thought, as material in character or from a divine source, as providing happiness or providing suffering. Truly, the actual experience of all those who conclusively realize the Self is as found in Ajata Vada, or the teaching of No-creation. The Self is unborn and imperishable, timeless and everlasting, locationless yet omnipresent, ever immutable, undergoing no modification or phase ever. It never gives rise to an "other." Of the nature of Being-Consciousness-Bliss, One without a second, of the nature of the Reality that ever is just as it is, it alone exists. This is Nonduality, to be realized directly by a thorough inquiry to know oneself. For those who are ardent in the pursuit of this inquiry, who are desirous of Self-Realization, and who are keenly aware of the inestimable, inner value of this teaching of Nonduality, the *Svatma-nirupanam* has been composed many centuries ago by Adi Sankara.

Sri Sankara commences this sacred work by offering salutations to his Guru, revealing how the glorious state of Self-Realization is simultaneously one of utmost humility, for it is devoid of ego. That which is the Guru, which is manifested as instruction and experienced as grace, is the power that destroys duality, which is a product of erroneous perception. The destruction of such ignorance, and its consequence of imagined duality, is Liberation from all bondage and suffering, which are unbearable as they run contrary to our true nature of Bliss, just as ignorance is contrary to Knowledge, and egoism is contrary to real Being. The sacred ash, mentioned by Sri Sankara and so familiar to those who are devoted to Siva, represents, as Sri Ramana Maharshi has explained, the residuum of unalloyed, nondual Being, or pure formless Existence, after the utter destruction of all the forms of illusion and delusion by the fire of Knowledge. In the second verse, Sri Sankara again praises his Guru, relating how pure compassion alone is the motivation for such sages to bestow their gracious teachings and loving assistance to destroy all doubts as to the nature of Reality, which is the true nature of oneself. The instruction is about the actual experience of Nonduality. This Nonduality signifies the indivisible, immutable, eternal Reality just as it is, which is the significance of the term "That" in such ageless Advaita Vedanta teachings as, "Tat Tvam Asi," meaning, "That you are."

Sri Sankara then proceeds to expound the Nondual teachings, setting the exposition in the form of a dialogue between a gracious, wise Guru and an ardently inquiring disciple. The disciple is described as scorched by the fire of samsara. Samsara is the repetitive cycle of birth and death, or illusion, characterized by sufferings of various kinds. Suffering is due to illusion, commencing with an "I," or individual, to which is attributed various forms of misidentification such as the mind, the senses, the body, and attachment to the things of the world. The illusion is the result of delusion, or ignorance, the fundamental basis of which is the ignorant notion of an existent, individual entity, or ego. That which is alone destructive of ignorance is Knowledge, and so by Self-Knowledge the disciple is enlightened by the Guru. That is, the Guru, who is the Self, reveals the same Absolute Self as the Self of the disciple. The Self then reposes in itself and is said to have realized itself. The ego has no part in such Realization, as something that is unreal cannot at all realize That which alone is ever real. The disciple's preparedness to absorb such teachings so as to realize the Self is constituted by what Sri Sankara refers to as "all practices." This may be understood as referring to sadhana chatushtaya, the four requisites or four means of spiritual practice. These are viveka or discrimination; vairagya or detachment; the sextet of essentials of sama or tranquility and peacefulness, dama or self-control, inclusive of control of the senses, uparati or renunciation and withdrawal from the external, titiksha or forbearance and fortitude, sraddha or sincere faith inclusive of the clear understanding and the unwavering determination to find out the Truth revealed by the scripture and the Guru in which one has faith, samadhana or profound, concentrated, formless meditation; and the fourth requisite of mumukshutva or the intense desire for Liberation. By an aspirant endowed with such practices, the teachings regarding the true definition of one's own Self are fully absorbed.

As did Sri Ramana Maharshi, Adi Sankara immediately reveals the fact of one's Existence. You are, and you know that you are. Such knowledge is identical with what is known, that is, your own Existence, and does not rely on any other means of knowing, such as thought or sense perception. It is not possible to doubt your existence, for if you did, surely the doubter's existence would still be taken for granted. The ultimate nature of that doubter can only be Existence itself. Existence is irrefutable. That Existence is Brahman, the solitary knower, of the nature of Consciousness. So, whether there is the idea of "I am" or the idea of "I am not," Brahman is, and that Brahman is alone the Self. The Self is only Brahman. The idea of oneself being different from Brahman in any manner or degree whatsoever is merely delusion, such delusion being the cause of suffering. The delusion is simply misidentification.

Thereafter, Sri Sankara describes how to discern the Self, utilizing discrimination to distinguish it from the sheaths that appear to cover it. It is a process, proceeding from gross to subtle, of freeing oneself from misidentification. This reveals one's real Being, which is Consciousness and which is Bliss itself. This Being-Consciousness-Bliss is before all and has no birth. It is after all and has no death. It is changeless and thus formless. It is always unaffected, and thus the Bliss of the Self is as ever-existent and invariable as Being itself is, as Consciousness itself is. Yet, it is only when one actually inquires to know oneself, liberating one's identity from the misidentification with all that constitutes the veiling sheaths, that the ever-effulgent Self shines in Knowledge of the Self.

In commencing an inquiry to know the Self, even if it first appears to the spiritual aspirant that there is nothing in his experience other than what constitutes the five sheaths, from the causal through the intellectual and mental to the prana and the body, there still exists one who is the knower, or experiencer, of these. All of these sheaths are objective to the Self, the innermost Consciousness. All of these are not one's actual Existence. The knower can never be a known or unknown object. The knower, the Self, is ever-existent and, being nonobjective, can only be formless without the least trace of any of the attributes of the known.

The object of experience will always correspond to the identity of the subject. So, if the subjective identity be that of the misidentification with the body, an objective world will appear to be the experience. Similarly, if the identity is composed of misidentification with the mind, thoughts, modes, and states of mind will be the corresponding object.

Upon inquiry, though, one recognizes the previously assumed subjective stand to be merely objective as well. This inquiry is revealed in the *Taittiriya Upanisad,* and the same inquiry to find the real Consciousness free of superimposed objective attributes of the sheaths is taught by Sri Sankara. Tracing the sheaths inwardly, the prana is the subject of the body, while prana is the object of the mind. The mind, though, is also an object of the intellect, and both are objective to the causal sheath. Still, there is one for whom all these are objective. Since that is interior to, or transcendent of, all that is gross and subtle, all that is manifest and even that which is unmanifest, all that can be conceived and even the absence of conception, there is nothing beyond it. That can never change its nature to become an object of experience. It is always existing as pure Consciousness, the self-effulgent illuminator of all. It knows all, yet none knows it, as the Self is always of the nature of pure, immutable Consciousness. It can neither be an object of something else nor can it be divided within itself as subject and object, "I" and "this." It may be regarded as that which experiences all, but nothing else experiences it. In saying so, Sri Sankara does not give any validity to the object of experience, nor yet to the notion of an individual experiencer, but rather emphasizes the reality of Consciousness. It can neither be perceived nor conceived, but is realized as itself by itself. That is the true Self, transcendent of the entire universe, dependent upon which is the universe, in which the universe appears, yet in which there is not actually ever a universe, since this Self is of the nature of homogeneous, undifferentiated, immutable Consciousness. Therefore, that alone is the sole-existent Reality for all eternity. Realizing the nonobjective nature of the Self is the way to Liberation from the bondage of illusion.

This Self is Brahman. Being the Reality and nonobjective, it is pure Existence of a completely formless nature. It is thus always attributeless. Therefore, as the Self is not this or that and never becomes this or that, but is always just Being, the Realization of the Self, or Self-Knowledge, which in nonduality must necessarily be of the identical nature as the Self which is realized or known, is only Being. It is not becoming or being this or that. It is simply Being, which is neither a thing nor an activity. This is clearly and abundantly taught by Sri Ramana Maharshi, and the very same is elucidated in verse eighteen of the *Svatmanirupanam* by Adi Sankara, the wondrous Acarya (Acharya, spiritual teacher) of Advaita Vedanta.

What is an object, be it gross or subtle, is not directly experienced. Such is experienced through some instrument or means of perception or conception. A gross object depends upon the body from which to perceive, the senses by which to perceive, the prana to enliven them, and the mind to cognize the senses. This occurs only in a particular state of mind, such as the waking state for waking state, objective experiences. A subtle object, that is, an object of thought, requires less to be experienced, but still requires a mind in a particular state. From a higher perspective, both what appears as gross and what appears as subtle, what appears as internal within the mind and what is imagined to be external due to misidentification with the body, are entirely within the mind. The waking state of mind constitutes the waking state experiences, just as a dreaming state of mind constitutes the dream state experiences. Misidentified within the state, the experiencer is perplexed and all of it seems real, though actually the invisible, indivisible Consciousness is alone real and all-pervading. However the experiences are viewed, they cannot wisely be regarded as directly experienced, yet Consciousness, which is one's very Existence, is always directly experienced or known, without being dependent on anything else in order to be or to be known.

The apparent, temporary existence of an object, anything regarded as "this," is contradicted by its nonexistence at another time. Everything born is subject to death. All that is created is also destroyed. The attributes of a body at one time are replaced by different or antithetical ones at another time. Thought along one line may be contradicted by contrary thinking at another time. All that is "this" is subject to change and destruction, and one who misidentifies with such does not find firm, lasting peace. Such peace is inherent in the changeless. The changeless is the Existence of the Self. It can never be disturbed by changeful phenomena and can never be contradicted by mental conception, for it is transcendent over matter and thought, is neither created nor destroyed, and is utterly nondependent. This Absolute Reality, is, as Sri Sankara states in verse 19, "not beyond Awareness." That is, it can be known as Consciousness itself. This is Supreme Knowledge, with no division into knower and known, and no separate relation or activity of knowing. All three are one and the same in this Nondual Self-Knowledge. It is Consciousness conscious of itself, yet not as an object. It is Existence reposing in itself, self-luminous and free of all misidentifications. Such is direct experience.

That Self is Brahman, which as the *Kenopanisad* (*Kena Upanishad*) declares, is known yet not known, which though not known (objectively) yet is known. In verse 20, Sri Sankara declares the definition of Brahman to be Reality-Knowledge-Infinity. It is Reality, for Being alone exists always, without modification. That which never undergoes modification, which is self-existent, and which never ceases to be, is Truth or Reality. Knowledge is as explained above and, as such, is pure Consciousness. Thus, Supreme Knowledge is Brahman. That which is without form and thus boundaryless, which is undifferentiated and thus partless and indivisible, which is timeless and eternal, and which has no limitations whatsoever is signified by "Infinity." That which is Reality-Knowledge-Infinity is alone the Self, for this Self is only Brahman.

In verses 20 and 64, Sri Sankara declares that satyam-jnanam-anantam, Truth-Knowledge-Infinity, is the very definition of Brahman, or the Supreme Self, thus graciously providing a description of the ineffable. The *Taittiriya Upanisad* declares the very same, and, in his commentary upon it, Sri Sankara elucidates the significance of these adjectives of Brahman. The Truth, or Reality, is that which never changes its nature, while the mutable should be recognized by the wise as unreal. If the real nature of Being is Consciousness, it is ever that, and thus the nature of the knower can never become other than what it is or bear any of the attributes of the known. Knowledge signifies

Consciousness itself, which, being formless and egoless, is not an individual knower. The Knowledge is, therefore, transcendent of both knower and known, and it is thus not the relation of those assumed poles, or dualistic cognition. If the Self would be regarded as an individual knower, it would be limited, and, therefore, Liberation would become impossible. The Knowledge that is Liberation is free of such a false assumption of individuality. Similarly, if the Self would be regarded as the known, there would need to be another to know it, but there is no one else to know the Self. The Self is not inert, and it is the experience of all that Consciousness is the most interior, the true meaning of "I," and does not require another to know it. Furthermore, in that commentary, Sri Sankara declares that Consciousness is the unchanging Reality and the unlimited, for it is neither the known nor the knower just mentioned. So, it is all-knowing, and the all-knowing is the all-blissful. That is, the Self is the Consciousness that knows and is the bliss of all beings everywhere for all time. Finally, Sri Sankara declares that the nature of Infinity is to be "not separate from anything," having no other. The Self is infinite in terms of space because it is not born of anything, having no form. It is infinite in time because it not created, but ever is. It is infinite in "substance" because it is identical with all. A differentiated thing is limited. Likewise, a differentiated idea is limited by both time and other ideas, as well as by its own form. The Self, though, is undifferentiated and thus limitless. That Self is Brahman, known to be the cause of all things, time, space, and all else. It is the cause of infinite space and is all-pervading. It is not a thing or a product of anything else and is without end in terms of time. Because there is nothing different from the Self, the Self is infinite in "substance." That Truth-Knowledge-Infinity is Reality and is absolute.

With misidentification with the sheaths, the nature of the Self is veiled. Mistaken to be an individual limited to the body and the mind, the Supreme is then seen as the Lord, as explained in verse 21. The individual being, or jiva, seems different from the Lord, or Isvara. They seem different in their attributes, and their attributes are regarded as determining their nature. In such ignorance, the jiva (individual) is assumed to be completely different in nature (unqualified duality), different with something of the Lord, who is the source, within the jiva (qualified duality), or similar in nature but with some difference such as magnitude, power, knowledge, etc. (qualified nonduality). With the negation of the misidentifications constituting the limitations of the jiva, the differences utterly vanish, being unreal. The one Self that had appeared as the Lord and the individual is realized just as it truly is, without any distinctions. The absence of the individual leaves only the Self, the Absolute, existing without any duality whatsoever. This is unqualified nonduality, or pure Advaita.

From the worldly-minded perspective, when all is seen as subject to change and contradiction, being perishable and unstable, it may seem that there is nothing absolutely real, nothing truly existing. If, instead, one wisely inquires to know oneself, one finds the Self to be beyond all that is subject to change. The Self and its Knowledge are most certainly beyond the worldly viewpoint. What is beyond all that is changeful and not subject to contradiction is Brahman. This is seen by the seers of Truth, by the rishis (sages) of the *Veda-s* and throughout all time. Sri Sankara brings forth not newly appearing ideas, for what appears will disappear, but rather elucidates eternal Truth. Always, the nature of the Self is the same, and that Self is the Self of all. Always, the suffering of living beings is caused only by ignorance characterized by misidentification, and always freedom from ignorance and suffering is by Knowledge, the Knowledge of the Self. Always the Reality, which is Brahman, is as it is. As it was, so it is, and so it will be always.

Though the Self exists always, shining as never-diminished Consciousness, the seeker of Self-Realization must reflect and deeply meditate upon the spiritual Truth expressed in the aphorisms of the wise sages, the teachings regarding the Self being That, in order to realize it. Otherwise, this Absolute Self seems to remain beyond the scope of one's experience, even though it is one's very Existence. By a deep inquiry into the meaning of the teaching, inquiring to know

"Who am I?" and by the Grace of the Master, which is beyond measure, Sri Sankara declares, one attains "a direct Awareness, in an instant, of the Self." The Knowledge of the Self is not time-bound. The Self, itself, neither comes nor goes, and its Realization, therefore, can never be quick or slow, for time does not exist in the Self. Moreover, it would be ridiculous to define or attempt to measure the Realization, which is of the nature of Reality and not an event that would occur to some individual, by the measurements and definitions of the unreal. In addition, the Reality of the Self is ever present, and, the moment ignorance is removed, it is known to be there without any delay. Whenever ignorance is removed, to the extent it is removed, to that extent the Self shines unobscured. When the superimposition is negated, That which truly exists and which was the substrate of the superimposed, alone remains. Since That was existing the whole time, both during the imagined bondage and in the revealed Liberation, it is not an attainment, and the Realization, being nondual and thus of the identical nature, is not an attainment, though all illusion and the sufferings of samsara are abolished. In his commentary upon the *Taittiriya Upanisad,* Sri Sankara says that the Self does not truly fall into the categories of attainment and non-attainment, realization and non-realization, as if there were different states for the Self. The Self is itself—in its own state always, as the Maharshi has declared—and the ego, being unreal, cannot have a real state. Sri Sankara states that one cannot attain oneself, for the Self is unlimited and identical with all, so Realization consists of the discovery through Knowledge of what is actually always true, just as, in the proverbial story of the tenth man, no one was lost or regained, but there was relief from all concern when right Knowledge dawned. Therefore, certitude of Knowledge is what is needed, while depth of inquiry is the means for it. Grace is ever present and is experienced proportionate to one's diving within. Therefore, Sankara has said in this *Svatmanirupanam*, "… reflecting upon the meaning of the aphorism, by the greatness of the Grace of the Master, one attains a direct Awareness, in an instant, of the Self."

The aspirant is blessed with the instruction of, "You are That." Prior to Self-inquiry, the "you" (that is, one's sense of "I") is confounded with the body, the senses, and the mind. Consequently, the "I" is considered to be an experiencer and the performer of the activities of the body, as explained in verse 25. As for "That," it is considered to be the omniscient Absolute, the very cause of the entire universe, which is truly Consciousness. Upon Self-inquiry, the Self is recognized as the Witness, which is Consciousness that is distinct from the body, the senses, the mind, and the ego. As for That, it is known by direct experience as immaculate Consciousness, which has no conditioning of any kind ever, as indestructible, as being without duality or anything else whatsoever, and as transcendent of the universe. With such inquiry, one arrives at true Knowledge by emphasis upon Consciousness itself, discarding the apparently different or contradictory attributes of the "I" and the Absolute ("That"). Since the most ancient times, the sacred Knowledge of the most profound wisdom has been taught by revealing the identity of the "I" and the "That." The instruction is "That you are," and the "are" or identity can be realized by the inquiry that reveals what the "I" truly is. Thus, by the inquiry, "Who am I?" is the profound Knowledge of the Self realized, and abidance in this Knowledge is freedom from all sorrow.

In verses 39 through 43, Adi Sankara extols the importance of the Guru, pointing out that purity of mind, performing religious practices such as rites, and engaging in other spiritual activities will not in themselves suffice for the highest good. In the relationship with the Guru, which is not a relationship as between two embodied beings, there occurs the dissolution of the ego of the disciple. The Guru abides as Brahman itself, the impersonal, bodiless, egoless Self, with no confusion regarding the Truth. By the Guru's wise, compassionate, gracious instruction, the disciple loses his individual identity, or ego. That which the Guru is, That which is the Self, That which is Brahman, alone remains. Next, Sri Sankara extols the *Veda-s*, proclaiming them to be the very pronouncements of the Supreme Lord and of a beginningless nature. This beginningless Knowledge is the Knowledge of the eternal, Absolute

Self, which is beginningless, and this Supreme Lord is none other than the Self itself. Specifically, Sri Sankara refers to that portion of the *Veda-s* that treats of the Supreme Knowledge, which is Nonduality and of which this *Svatmanirupanam* is a reiteration. Indeed, Sri Sankaracharya states that all that is written concerning this Knowledge, no matter how wonderful, is only a restatement of the original Knowledge.

For one desirous of the Supreme Knowledge of the Self, this reliance on the *Veda-s* is one of four crucial validations of one's understanding, as described by Sri Sankara in other works of his. The first, already mentioned, is the sruti, or the *Veda-s*. The second is smriti, or "remembered works" constituted of those scriptural or spiritual texts that come after the *Veda-s*. The disciple may view his own Guru's instructions as belonging to what is mentioned thus far. The third is deep reasoning, which is of the nature of discrimination, the essence of which is inquiry to know the Self. The fourth is one's own direct experience. Only when one's knowledge coincides with all four of these criteria, validated by all four, can the knowledge be regarded as true. This safeguards the seeker from mistaking self-created ideas or transient experiences for Truth and from misinterpreting the holy texts, as well. The *Veda-s* provide the ancient root of eternal Truth, the smriti-s provide the details of instruction, discrimination and inquiry provide the clear understanding, and one's own direct experience ensures that such does not remain as indirect, objectified knowledge. In *Vivekacudamani, The Crest Jewel of Discrimination*, Sri Sankara describes these four validations as holy texts, deep reasoning inclusive of meditation on the Supreme, instruction by the Guru, and direct, inner experience.

Nonduality is Truth. Dualism is merely a superimposition upon the Truth. The Reality is never superimposed. Rather, the unreal, the illusory, is superimposed, through ignorance, upon the Reality, as Sri Sankara explains in verse 52. Therefore, utter Nonduality is not an idea superimposed upon a real duality. Rather, unreal duality is merely superimposed, by imagination, upon Nonduality. Nonduality is the Truth established by the *Veda-s* and other sacred texts that declare the Supreme Truth, such as this *Svatmanirupanam*. These holy books contain a sacred message that might not otherwise be understood. They do not confirm existing ignorance, but rather reveal Knowledge that transcends and destroys such ignorance. One does not require such holy works to learn of dualism, because one already knows of such dualism by worldly experience in the samsara. The texts are composed to reveal something not gained by worldly experience and not to be known by worldly means. That something is Nonduality. As long as duality subsists, suffering will be experienced. Such suffering is intolerable because it is contrary to one's true nature of Being-Consciousness-Bliss. For the sake of happiness, one seeks the true definition of oneself. With such Knowledge, one knows Being as it is, and in Nonduality, one is what one knows. Thus, there is the unalloyed, limitless Bliss of Being, which is as continuous and unending as ever-existent Being itself is.

The Self is blissful, Absolute Being, yet, in ignorance, it is assumed to be a limited individual entity, or jiva. This is described in verses 56 through 62. The jiva, being a product of ignorance, is unreal, or may be regarded as a misperception of what is real. If the individual entity, or ego, were really such, it would always be such, as a thing does not actually change its nature. If it is real, it is ever real. If it is unreal, it is ever unreal. The transient does not become the eternal, and the eternal does not become transient. The nonobjective does not become a thing, and an object does not become the transcendent Consciousness. The homogeneous, undifferentiated, and nondual does not become split, differentiated, and dual, and vice versa. The real Consciousness does not become an unreal thought, and an unreal thought does not become, or attain to, the real Consciousness. Therefore, if individuality be the real nature of the individual, it will always be so, but then there would be no Liberation possible, as it is agreed by all that Liberation is the egoless state. Without Liberation, there would be no permanent peace and happiness. A state lacking in peace and characterized by unhappiness runs contrary to one's nature. So, such peace and happiness are sought. They are to be found within. Within is the Self. The Self is real, and thus ever-existent. One need only know the Self as it truly is and not misconstrue it to be an ego-entity in order to abide in the lasting peace and happiness of the Absolute Reality, for ignorance regarding such is the cause of all that is of the nature of suffering and futility. Therefore, Self-Realization is what is necessary. The Self that is to be realized must be innately egoless. That Self will never change its nature. Its Realization, or Knowledge of itself, is the experience of permanent peace and happiness. What then is the individual? This is the inquiry to be made by the seeker of Self-Knowledge. Upon such inquiry, this falsely assumed individuality vanishes, leaving the residuum of egoless Being, which was the only real identity or Existence the entire time. The true nature of the individual is, thus, only the real Self, which has no attribute of individuality whatsoever.

By Knowledge alone does the misidentification with the body and the delusion of samsara vanish. This cannot be accomplished by any bodily means. Ignorance is not a production of the body, and Knowledge, also, is not a bodily production. Ignorance has no valid cause, though it seems to rise from the "I." Yet, when one inquires into this "I," its "I"-ness vanishes, being unreal, and along with it vanishes ignorance, which is unreal. As for true Knowledge, it inheres in the Self. The effects of ignorance cannot be reasonably considered its cause. The effect is the samsara, of which the misidentification with the body is a pivotal factor. If the effects be traced to their cause, and that causal "I" be inquired into, what remains is oneself, the Self, alone, one without a second.

Sri Sankara declares that Self-Knowledge alone is necessary. The path to such Knowledge consists of Knowledge, the primary means for which is the practice of Self-inquiry. That which is the active ingredient in any practice resulting in deeper spiritual experience is Knowledge. Without it, no deeper experience is forthcoming. Yet, Knowledge itself can stand alone. As stated in verse 70, it requires no other assistance, just as the brilliant sun does not require some other help to dispel darkness. The inquiry to know oneself is all-sufficient for the elimination of the darkness of ignorance and the revelation of the Absolute.

Sri Sankara proclaims that the relation between the objects of experience (inclusive of the world and thought, the gross and the subtle) and the real Existence is like that of an imagined snake superimposed upon a rope. The rope alone is, even when, in dim light, it is misperceived as a snake. The snake is never actually born, nor does it have any reality at all, other than that of the rope. The rope never changes its nature. It neither projects a snake nor changes into a snake. So it is with the Self and the imagination of anything else. This is the true purport of the essence of the *Veda-s* and all the other texts and teachings that declare the highest Truth.

In verses 72 and 73, Sri Sankara explains that, in relation to all that is objective, the Self is the silent witness. The witness is attributeless and formless. Its ultimate nature is pure Being, unmodified Consciousness, nondependent Bliss. In meditating upon the Self as the witness, no reality is to be attributed to the witnessed. The meditation is a return of happiness, identity, and reality to their true abode, and that is the uncreated Self. The witnessed is unreal, like a snake imagined where there is only a rope. As the rope alone exists and there never is really a snake, so it is with the Self and the non-Self. As the rope truly has no connection to the snake, that is to say the snake is only the rope though the rope is not at all ever a snake, so the unchanging Self is ever as it is and is never attached to unreal things.

In expedient teachings employed to assist the aspirant, maya, or illusion, is the reason given for the appearance of the Self as an experiencer, the performer of action, and such and the corresponding objects of such. However, as explained by Sri Sankara, maya itself does not actually exist. What is, is only Brahman, and nothing other than That ever comes to be. This Truth is seen by the seers of Truth, as the Real ever is and the unreal never is. Brahman is all that ever is. What seems to be a universe is only Brahman and not anything else. One who knows Brahman, therefore, knows all that there truly is, and this is true Knowledge. To aid the seeker, Sri

Sankara further teaches that same Brahman to be the cause of the universe, for, since the effect cannot be of a different nature than the cause, and since it is only illusion that makes it appear otherwise, such understanding leads to true Knowledge.

Verses 80 through 83 continue to instruct along these lines, revealing how all—the Guru, the disciple, and the entire universe—are only the Supreme Reality. Yet, in order to ensure that this profound instruction is not consumed within the context of the previous ignorant conception of the world being real in any way, he negates the idea that the universe is real. Viewed in highest Knowledge, the three statements, "The world is unreal," "Brahman alone is real," and "The universe is Brahman alone," all have the identical significance. This is to be known by an inner, experiential inquiry. Without such inquiry, these aphorisms, and how their meanings are identical, remain a mystery.

Between "I" and "this" is displayed all delusion. The direct means of realizing the Truth, the true definition of one's own Self, is to hold on to the "I" and inquire to determine what it is. The answer to such inquiry is never an objective conception. The only answer, as Sri Ramana Maharshi explained, is the nature of the inquirer himself. From verse 84 onward, Sri Sankara, speaking as the Guru, describes in detail this essential inquiry into the "I," revealing the Self's freedom from the body, senses, ego, and all else. After instructing in the manner of inquiry, he again reveals the ajata (no-creation) teaching of complete Nonduality, going beyond even the apparent distinctions of ignorance and knowledge, making clear that Brahman, the Self, alone is. The Guru's instruction finishes with descriptions of the sublime, exalted, indivisible state of the realized sages who know this unalterable Truth without an alternative.

Thereupon, in the context of the dialogue, the disciple, having deeply meditated upon all that was taught by the Guru until no more contradictions to it could possibly arise in his mind, describes his own direct experience. This portion of the text is cast in the first person, for the "I" has been realized as the true Self, and nothing else remains of his "I." The aspirant who reads these lines should observe that these statements in the "first person" are made by one who has already realized the Truth of them by deep inquiry, and they are presented as such. It would not be wise to use such statements as a surrogate for the actual practice of inquiry, for such would not eliminate the ego. When the ego is gone, its illusory existence destroyed by the Knowledge of the Self, what is described in the remainder of the *Svatmanirupanam* is one's own direct experience, the natural state. The descriptions are those of complete detachment, of the vast and universal view of the Self, and of identity with Being-Consciousness-Bliss. In verse 110, the term, "uhapoha" is customarily interpreted as positive and negative reasoning or consideration of the pros and cons of a topic being contemplated. In the verse, "inquiry" is added, so that the interpretation is that of an inquiry into the pros and cons or an inquiry using positive and negative reasoning. These terms may also be understood as comprehending, reasoning, and inquiry, which is the process of absorbing the teachings of Nonduality; or as examination, removing, and inquiry, which is descriptive of the process of examination of ignorance composed of misidentification and attachment, the removal of such, and the inquiry into the nature of what remains of the "I" upon such removal. Thereafter, the disciple continues to describe, in the "first person" indicative of direct experience, the nature of the Self in both cosmic and attributeless terms, as the infinite, as the eternal, as that which is all, as the essence, and as the utterly transcendent. He abides as identical with the Self and its Realization. No more is there the conception of a self to realize, a Self to be realized, the movement toward Realization and a state of Realization. Being alone is, and it is the Self, free of the division of realizer and realized. Being is itself the Realization. Toward the conclusion of his description, the disciple glorifies the Guru again and again, for there is in him no ego to claim his experience.

The *Svatmanirupanam* concludes with a re-statement of the ajata vada (teaching of no-creation, no-birth), the Truth of which is realized by all who abide in Self-Knowledge—the state of Kaivalyam, the state of being That which alone is—as well as a final exhortation for you, who are reading this, to deeply reflect on these teachings about your own true Self.

In order to aid the seeker in obtaining a thorough comprehension, wherever alternative translations of a word or phrase are possible, such has been included in the word-by-word translation, though, in a few instances, they have been incorporated into the final, running English translation, as well. Terms and phrases in parenthesis are supplied to clarify the meaning of the preceding word or phrase, while terms and phrases placed in brackets indicate an insertion by the translators considered necessary to render the passage comprehensible in English. As the two editions of Sri Sankara's Sanskrit text that served as the original basis of the present English text differ at points, the translators have chosen those portions of each that seemed most consistent with the rest of the text. With those passages in which the two editions differ significantly and the text would seem to allow for either meaning to be appropriate, both versions have been given in the translation. Any mistakes that may appear herein are entirely the fault of the assistant translator and do not reflect any flaw in the flawless original text or in the meticulous, devoted, selfless work of the primary translator, the late Dr. H. Ramamoorthy.

May this English translation of the *Svatmanirupanam* serve the same intention of the Sanskrit original composed by the wondrous sage, Adi Sankaracharya. May He be pleased with what is here. May this be an offering to Him.

May this presentation of the ancient teachings pertaining to the inquiry resulting in Self-Knowledge serve the same intention as the liberating teachings of this inquiry by my ever-gracious Guru, Bhagavan Sri Ramana Maharshi. May He be pleased with what is here. May this be an offering to Him.

May this be an offering to Brahman.

1

श्रीगुरुचरणद्वन्द्वं वन्देऽहं मथितदुःसहद्वन्द्वम् ।
भ्रान्तिग्रहोपशान्तिं पांसुमयं यस्य भसितमातनुते ॥ १ ॥

śrī-guru-caraṇa-dvandvaṁ vande'haṁ mathita-
duḥsaha-dvandvam
bhrānti-grahopaśāntiṁ pāṁsu-mayaṁ yasya bhasitam-
ātanute

sri guru **the revered guru** carana **feet** dvandvam **pair** vande-aham **I bow to/I salute** mathita **destroying** dus-saha **unbearable** dvandvam **pair of opposites**[1] bhranti-graha **the (malefic) planet of erroneous perception** upasantim **allaying** pamsu-mayam **full of dust** yasya **of which** bhasitam **ashes** atanute **causes**

I bow to the revered guru's pair of feet,
Which destroy the unbearable pair of opposites,
The dust of which is the ash allaying
The (malefic) planet of erroneous perception.

---

[1] *Duality, such as happiness and sorrow.*

2

देशिकवरं दयालुं वन्देऽहं निहतनिखिलसंदेहम् ।

यच्चरणद्वयमद्वयमनुभवमुपदिशति तत्पदस्यार्थम् ॥ २ ॥

deśikavaraṁ dayāluṁ vande'haṁ nihata-nikhila-
saṁdeham
yac-caraṇa-dvayam-advayam-anubhavam-upadiśati
tat-padasy-ārtham

desika-varam **the excellent guru** dayalum **the compassionate** vande-aham **I bow to** nihata-nikhila-sandeham **who destroys all doubts** yat-carana-dvayam **whose feet** advayam-anubhavam **the non-dual experience** upadisati **instructs** tat-padasya-artham **the meaning of the word "That"**

To the excellent guru, the compassionate (one),
I bow,
Who destroys all doubts,
Whose feet instruct one in the nondual experience,
The meaning of the word "That."

3

संसारदावपावकसंतप्तः सकलसाधनोपेतः ।
स्वात्मनिरूपणनिपुणैर्वाक्यैः शिष्यः प्रबोध्यते गुरुणा ॥ ३ ॥

saṁsāra-dāva-pāvaka-saṁtaptaḥ sakala-sādhanopetaḥ
svātma-nirūpaṇa-nipuṇair-vākyaiḥ śiṣyaḥ prabodhyate
guruṇā

samsara-dava-pavaka **the forest fire of samsara (the birth-death cycle)** samptaptah **scorched** sakala-sadhana-upetah **possessed of all practices** sv-atma **or** su-atma **one's Self/one's own Self/the true Self** nirupana **definition** nipunaih-vakyaih **by accurate perfect words** sisyah **disciple** prabodhyate **is enlightened/instructed** guruna **by the Guru**

Scorched by the forest fire of samsara,
Possessed of all practices,
The disciple is enlightened by the Guru
In perfect, accurate words, as to the definition of
one's own (the true) Self.

4

अस्ति स्वयमित्यस्मिन्नर्थे कस्यास्ति संशयः पुंसः ।
अत्रापि संशयश्चेत्संशयिता यः स एव भवसि त्वम् ॥ ४ ॥

asti svayam-ity-asminn-arthe kasyāsti saṁśayaḥ
puṁsaḥ
atrāpi saṁśayaś-cet-saṁśayitā yaḥ sa eva bhavasi tvam

asti svayam-iti **that oneself exists** asmin-arthe **in this fact** kasya **for whom** asti **exists** samsayah **doubt** pumsah **for a person** atrapi **even in this** samsayah-cet **if there be doubt** samsayita-yah **he who has the doubt** sa-eva **he indeed** bhavasi **are** tvam **you**

"Oneself exists"—in this fact
For whom does a doubt exist?
Even in this, if there be doubt,
He who has the doubt, indeed, you are.

5

नाहमिति वेत्ति योऽसौ सत्यं ब्रह्मैव वेत्ति नास्तीति ।

अहमस्मीति विजानन्ब्रह्मैवासौ स्वयं विजानाति ॥ ५ ॥

nāham-iti vetti yo'sau satyaṁ brahmaiva vetti nāstīti
aham-asmīti vijānan-brahmaiv-āsau svayaṁ vijānāti

na-aham **"I am not"** iti **thus** vetti **knows** yah-asau **he who** satyam **truly** brahma-eva **Brahman indeed** vetti **knows** na-asti-iti **that "He is not"** aham-asmi **"I am"** iti-vijanan **knowing thus** brahma-eva **Brahman indeed** asau **he** svayam **himself** vijanati **knows**

When one knows that "I am not,"
Truly, Brahman, indeed, it is that knows he is not;
Knowing that "I am,"
Brahman, indeed, it is that knows himself thus.

6

ब्रह्म त्वमेव तस्मान्नाहं ब्रह्मेति मोहमात्रमिदम् ।
मोहेन भवति भेदः क्लेशाः सर्वे भवन्ति तन्मूलाः ॥ ६ ॥

brahma tvam-eva tasmān-nāhaṁ brahmeti moha-
mātram-idam
mohena bhavati bhedaḥ kleśāḥ sarve bhavanti tan-
mūlāḥ

brahma tvam-eva **Brahman is only yourself** tasmat **hence** na-aham brahma-iti **that "I am not Brahman"** moha-matram **is only delusion** idam **this** mohena **by delusion** bhavati **comes into being** bhedah **difference** klesah **sorrows** sarve **all** bhavanti **come into being/are** tat-mulah **rooted in that**

Brahman is only yourself.
Hence, "I am not Brahman"—this is only delusion.
Difference comes into being from delusion;
All sorrows are rooted in that.

7

न क्लेशपञ्चकमिदं भजते कृतकोशपञ्चकविवेकः ।
अत एव पञ्च कोशान्कुशलधियः संततं विचिन्वन्ति ॥ ७ ॥

na kleśa-pañcakam-idaṁ bhajate kṛta-kośa-pañcaka-
vivekaḥ
ata eva pañca kośān-kuśala-dhiyaḥ saṁtataṁ
vicinvanti

klesa-pancakam-idam **this pentad of troubles** na-bhajate **does not experience** krta-kosa-pancaka-vivekah **he who has the discrimination regarding the pentad of sheaths** ata-eva **hence it is** panca-kosan **the pentad of sheaths** kusala-dhiyah **persons of skillful intellect** samtatam **ever** vicinvanti **investigate**

The pentad of troubles[1] is not experienced by one
Who has discrimination of the pentad of sheaths.
Hence it is that persons of skillful intellect
Ever investigate the pentad of sheaths.

---

[1] *Ignorance (avidyā), egoism (asmitā), attachment (rāga), aversion (dveṣa) and the clinging to life or tenacious desire (abhineveśa).*

8

अन्नप्राणमनोमयविज्ञानानन्दपञ्चकोशानाम् ।

एकैकान्तरभाजां भजति विवेकात्प्रकाशतामात्मा ॥ ८ ॥

anna-prāṇa-manomaya-vijñān-ānanda-pañca-kośānām
ekaik-āntara-bhājāṁ bhajati vivekāt-prakāśatām-ātmā

anna **food** prana **prana (the vital airs)** mano-maya **of the nature of the mind** vijnana **intellect, knowledge** ananda **bliss** panca-kosan **(this) pentad of sheaths** eka-eka-antara-bhajam **existing one inside another** bhajati **experiences** vivekat **from discrimination** prakasatam **the shining** atma **the Self**

The pentad of sheaths of food, prana,
Mind, [intellectual] knowledge and bliss,
Existing one inside another, from discrimination,
The shining Self experiences.

9

वपुरिदमन्नमयाख्यः कोशो नात्मा जडो घटप्रायः ।
प्रागुत्पत्तेः पश्चात्तदभावस्यापि दृश्यमानत्वात् ॥ ९ ॥

vapur-idam-anna-mayākhyaḥ kośo nātmā jaḍo ghaṭaprāyaḥ
prāg-utpatteḥ paścāt-tad-abhāvasyāpi dṛśyamānatvāt

vapuh-idam **this body** annamaya-akhyah **known as of the nature of food** kosah **(is) a sheath** na-atma **not the Self** jadah **inert** ghata-prayah **like a pot** prag-utpatteh **having an origin** pascat **later** tad-abhavasya-api **and its ceasing to exist** drsya-manatvat **being an object of perception**

This body, known to be of the nature of food,
Is a sheath, not the Self, for it is inert like a pot,
Having an origin earlier, ceasing to exist later,
And being an object of perception.

10

कोशः प्राणमयोऽयं वायुविशेषो वपुष्यवच्छिन्नः ।
अस्य कथमात्मता स्यात्क्षुत्तृष्णाभ्यामुपेयुषः पीडाम् ॥ १० ॥

kośaḥ prāṇa-mayo'yaṁ vāyu-viśeṣo vapuṣy-avacchinnaḥ
asya katham-ātmatā syāt-kṣut-tṛṣṇābhyām-upeyuṣaḥ pīḍām

kosam prana-mayah-ayam **this sheath of the nature of prana (vital airs)** vayu-visesah **is a kind of air** vapusi **inside the body** avacchinnah **delimited** asya **for this** katham **how** atmata **Self-hood** syat **can be?** ksut-trsnabhyam **by hunger and thirst** upeyusah **connected with** pidam **affliction**

This sheath of the nature of prana,
A kind of air inside the body and delimited by the body—
How can there be Self-hood for this,
Connected, as it is, with the affliction of hunger and thirst?

11

कुरुते वपुष्यहंतां गेहादौ यः करोति ममतां च ।

रागद्वेषविधेयो नासावात्मा मनोमयः कोशः ॥ ११ ॥

kurute vapuṣy-ahaṁtāṁ gehādau yaḥ karoti
mamatāṁ ca
rāga-dveṣa-vidheyo nāsāv-ātmā manomayaḥ kośaḥ

kurute **creates** vapusi **in the body** ahamtam **"I-ness" (the sense of I)** geha-adau yah **in regard to house and others which** karoti **creates** mamatam-ca **"my-ness" also (the sense of "mine" also)** raga-dvesa-vidheyah **being subject to likes and dislikes** na-asau-atma **this is not the Self** manah-mayah kosah **the sheath of the nature of the mind**

Creating the sense of "I" in regard to the body,
Creating the sense of "mine" in regard to the house
and others,
Subject to likes and dislikes,
This, the sheath of the nature of the mind, is not the
Self.

12

सुप्तौ स्वयं विलीना बोधे व्याप्ता कलेबरं सकलम् ।
विज्ञानशब्दवाच्या चित्प्रतिबिम्बो न बुद्धिरप्यात्मा ॥ १२ ॥

suptau svayaṁ vilīnā bodhe vyāptā kalebaraṁ
sakalam
vijñāna-śabda-vācyā cit-prati-bimbo na buddhirapy-
ātmā

suptau **in the deep sleep state** svayam vilina **disappearing into itself/merging into itself** bodhe **on awakening** vyapta **pervading** kalebaram sakalam **the entire body** vijnana-sabda-vacya **known by the name of intellect** cit-prati-bimbah **the reflection of Consciousness** na buddhih-api **intellect also is not** atma **the Self**

In deep sleep, disappearing into itself,
On awakening, pervading the entire body,
Known by the name of [the sheath of] intellect,
This reflection of Consciousness, too, is not the Self.

13

सुप्तिगतैः सुखलेशैरभिमनुते यः सुखी भवामीति ।
आनन्दकोशनामा सोऽहंकारः कथं भवेदात्मा ॥ १३ ॥

supti-gataiḥ sukhaleśair-abhimanute yaḥ sukhī
bhavāmīti
ānanda-kośa-nāmā so'haṁkāraḥ kathaṁ bhaved-ātmā

supti gataih **while in the deep sleep state** sukha-lesaih **by snatches of happiness** abhimanute-yah **that which (he who) believes** sukhi-bhavami-iti **that I am happy** ananda-kosa-nama **named the sheath of bliss** sah-ahankarah **that ego** katham **how** bhaved **can it be** atma **the Self?**

That which believes, "I am happy,"
In the snatches of happiness while in the deep sleep state,
Named as the sheath of bliss—
How can that ego be the Self?

14

यः स्फुरति बिम्बभूतः स भवेदानन्द एव सकलात्मा ।
प्रागूर्ध्वमपि च सत्त्वादविकारित्वादबाध्यमानत्वात् ॥ १४ ॥

yaḥ sphurati bimba-bhūtaḥ sa bhaved-ānanda eva sakalātmā
prāg-ūrdhvam-api ca sattvād-avikāritvād-abādhyamānatvāt

yah sphurati **that which shines** bimba-bhutah **being the (original) being** sah bhavet-ananda eva t**hat bliss indeed will be** sakala-atma **the Self of all** prag **before** urdhvam-api **and later** ca **also** sattvat **by being existent** avikaritvat **by its changelessness** abadhyamanatvat **by not being affected [by anything else]**

What shines as being the original being,
That indeed is the Bliss, the Self of all,
Because it is existent before and after,
Being changeless and not affected [by anything else].

15

अन्नमयादेरस्मादपरं यदि नानुभूयते किंचित् ।

अनुभवितान्नमयादेरस्तीत्यस्मिन्न कश्चिदपलापः ॥ १५ ॥

anna-mayāder-asmād-aparaṁ yadi nānubhūyate
kiṁcit
anubhavit-ānnamayāder-astīty-asmin-na kaścid-
apalāpaḥ

anna maya adeh **(the sheaths) of the nature of food and others** asmad aparam **beyond this** yadi na anubhuyate **if not experienced** kimcit **anything** anubhavita **the experiencer** anna maya adeh **of (the sheaths) of the nature of food and others** asti **exists** iti **thus** asmin **in this** na kascit apalapah **there is no detraction**

Beyond the annamaya (of the nature of food)
[sheath]and others,
If nothing else be experienced,
There is no detraction from this—that
There exists an experiencer of the annamaya
and others.

16

स्वयमेवानुभवत्वाद्यद्यप्येतस्य नानुभाव्यत्वम् ।

सकृदप्यभावशङ्का न भवेद्बोधस्वरूपसत्तायाः ॥ १६ ॥

svayamev-ānubhavatvād-yadyapy-etasya
nānubhāvyatvam
sakṛdapy-abhāva-śaṅkā na bhaved-bodha-svarūpa-
sattāyāḥ

svayam-eva **by itself** anubhavatvat **experiencing** yadyapi **although** etasya na-anubhavyam **it cannot be experienced** sakrd-api **even once** abhava-sanka **the doubt of nonexistence** na bhavet **will not arise/will not exist** bodha-svarupa-sattayah **of the Reality, which is of the nature of Knowledge (Consciousness)**

Though it, of itself, experiences,
It cannot be experienced;
There can never even once be a doubt of
nonexistence
Of the Reality, which is of the nature of Knowledge.

17

अनुभवति विश्वमात्मा विश्वेनासौ न चानुभूयेत ।

न खलु प्रकाश्यतेऽसौ विश्वमशेषं प्रकाशयन्भानुः ॥ १७ ॥

anubhavati viśvam-ātmā viśven-āsau na cānubhūyeta
na khalu prakāśyate'sau viśvam-aśeṣaṁ prakāśayan-
bhānuḥ

anubhavati **experiences** visvam **the universe** atma **the Self** visvena **by the universe** asau **this (Self)** na ca anubhuyeta **but is not experienced** na khalu **not indeed** prakasyate **illumined** asau **this (sun)** visvam **this universe/all else** asesam **fully** prakasayan **illuminating** bhanuh **the sun**

The Self experiences the universe,
But this (Self) is not experienced by the universe.
The sun fully illumines all else,
But is itself not illumined, indeed.

18

तदिदं तादृशमीदृशमेतावत्तावदिति च यन्न भवेत् ।
ब्रह्म तदित्यवधेयं नो चेद्विषयो भवेत्परोक्षं च ॥ १८ ॥

tad-idaṁ tādṛśam-īdṛśam-etāvat-tāvad-iti ca yan-na
bhavet
brahma tad-ity-avadheyaṁ no ced-viṣayo bhavet-
parokṣaṁ ca

tat **that** idam **this** tadrsam **like that** idrsam **like this** etavat **this much** tavat **that much** iti ca **and thus** yat **that which** na bhavet **will not be** brahma **Brahman** tat **That** iti **thus** avadheyam **should be understood** no cet **if not** visayah bhavet-paroksam ca **and the thing will be beyond awareness**

That, this, like that, like this, this much, that much,
and thus—
That which will not be so
Should be understood to be Brahman;
Otherwise, it would be an object and not directly
experienced.

19

इदमिदमिति प्रतीते वस्तुनि सर्वत्र बाध्यमानेऽपि।

अनिदमबाध्यं तत्त्वं सत्त्वादेतस्य न च परोक्षत्वम् ॥ १९ ॥

idam-idam-iti pratīte vastuni sarvatra bādhyamāne'pi
anidam-abādhyaṁ tattvaṁ sattvād-etasya na ca
parokṣatvam

idam-idam **"this," "this"** iti **thus** pratite **believed** vastuni **objects** sarvatra **everywhere** badhyamane api **even though (they) can be disturbed/contradicted** an-idam **not this** a-badhyam **undisturbable** tattvam **Reality, Truth** sattvat **because it exists** etasya **for this** na ca paroksatvam **not being beyond awareness/ direct experience**

Even though objects everywhere
Believed as "this," "this" can be disturbed
(or contradicted),
Reality, because of Existence, is undisturbable
(or uncontradictable)
And is not beyond Awareness (direct experience).

20

नावेद्यमपि परोक्षं भवति ब्रह्म स्वयंप्रकाशत्वात् ।
सत्यं ज्ञानमनन्तं ब्रह्मेत्येतस्य लक्षणं प्रथते ॥ २० ॥

nāvedyam-api parokṣaṁ bhavati brahma svayaṁ-
prakāśatvāt
satyaṁ-jñānam-anantaṁ brahmety-etasya lakṣaṇaṁ
prathate

avedyam-api na paroksam bhavati **though not knowable is not beyond awareness** brahma **Brahman** svayam-prakasatvat **because of being self-luminous** satyam-jnanam-anantam brahma **Brahman is Reality, Knowledge, Infinity** iti **thus** etasya laksanam **its definition** prathate **is expressed**

Brahman, though not knowable (intellectually)
Is not beyond Awareness, being self luminous.
Brahman is Reality, Knowledge, Infinity.
Thus is expressed its definition.

21

सति कोशशक्त्युपाधौ संभवतस्तस्य जीवतेश्वरते ।

नो चेत्तयोरभावाद्विगतविशेषं विभाति निजरूपम् ॥ २१ ॥

sati kośa-śakty-upādhau saṁbhavatas-tasya jīvat-
eśvarate
no cet-tayor-abhāvād-vigata-viśeṣaṁ vibhāti nija-
rūpam

sati kosa-sakti-upadhau **if there is conditioning by the power of the sheaths** sambhavatah **come into being** tasya **for it (the Self)** jivata-isvarate **jiva-hood and isvara-hood (the states of being jiva and isvara) (the state of being an individual and the state of being the Lord)** no cet **if not** tayoh abhavat **because of their nonexistence** vigata-visesam **without distinctions** vibhati **shines** nija-rupam **the real nature**

If there is conditioning by the power of the sheaths,
The states of being jiva[1] and Isvara[2] come into being
for the Self.
If not, in their absence (because of their
nonexistence),
The Self shines in its real nature, without
distinctions.

---

[1] *Individual.*

[2] *The Lord.*

22

सति सकलदृश्यबाधे न किमप्यस्तीति लोकसिद्धं चेत् ।
यन्न किमपीति सिद्धं ब्रह्म तदेवेति वेदतः सिद्धम् ॥ २२ ॥

sati sakala-dṛśya-bādhe na kimapy-astīti loka-siddhaṁ
cet
yan-na kimapīti siddhaṁ brahma tad-eveti vedataḥ
siddham

sati sakala-drsya-badhe **if all that is seen is subject to contradiction** na kim-api-asti **nothing at all exists** iti loka-siddham cet **if thus is the common/worldly decision** yat-na kim-api-iti siddham **that which is determined to be none (of these) at all** brahma tad-eva **that indeed is Brahman** iti **thus** vedatah siddham **is the determination by the Veda-s**

If all that is seen is subject to contradiction,
Nothing at all exists—if thus is the worldly
decision,
That which is determined to be none (of these) at all,
Is, indeed, Brahman—thus is the determination by
the Veda-s.

23

एवमपि विरहितानां तत्त्वमसीत्यादिवाक्यचिन्तनया ।
प्रतिभात्येष परोक्षवदात्मा प्रत्यक्प्रकाशमानोऽपि ॥ २३ ॥

evam-api virahitānāṁ tat-tvam-asīty-ādi-vākya-
cintanayā
pratibhāty-eṣa parokṣavad-ātmā pratyak-
prakāśamāno'pi

evam api **though this is so** virahitanam **to those devoid of** tat-tvam-asi-iti-adi **"That you are" and such** vakya-cintanaya **reflection on the aphorisms** prabhati **seems** esah **this** paroksavat **as if beyond awareness** atma **the Self** pratyak-prakasamanah-api **though shining inwardly**

Though this is so, to those devoid of reflection
On aphorisms such as "That you are,"
This Self seems as if beyond awareness (invisible),
Though shining inwardly.

24

तस्मात्पदार्थशोधनपूर्वं वाक्यस्य चिन्तयन्नर्थम् ।
देशिकदयाप्रभावादपरोक्षयति क्षणेन चात्मानम् ॥ २४ ॥

tasmāt-padārtha-śodhana-pūrvaṁ vākyasya cintayann-
artham
deśika-dayā-prabhāvād-aparokṣayati kṣaṇena
cātmānam

tasmat **therefore** pada-artha-sodhana-purvam **by an inquiry into the meaning of the words** vakyasya **of the aphorism** cintayan-artham **reflecting upon the meaning** desika-daya-prabhavat **by the greatness of the Grace of the Master** aparoksayati **one attains a direct Awareness** ksanena ca **and, in an instant** atmanam **of the Self**

Therefore, by an inquiry into the meaning of the
words,
And reflecting upon the meaning of the aphorism,
By the greatness of the Grace of the Master, one
attains
A direct Awareness, in an instant, of the Self.

25

देहेन्द्रियादिधर्मानात्मन्यारोपयन्नभेदेन ।
कर्तृत्वाद्यभिमानी बोधः स्यात्त्वंपदस्य वाच्योऽर्थः ॥ २५ ॥

dehendriyādi-dharmān-ātmany-āropayann-abhedena
kartṛtvādy-abhimānī bodhaḥ syāt-tvaṁ-padasya
vācyo'rthaḥ

deha-indriya-adi **the body, the senses and such** dharman **functions** atmani **on the Self** aropayan **superimposing** abhedena **without differentiation** kartrtva-adi **doership and such** abhimani **experiencer** bodhah **knowledge** syat **could be** tvam padasya **of the word "you"** vacya-arthah **the ostensible meaning**

Superimposing on the Self, without differentiation,
The functions of the body, senses, and such,
The knowledge of being the experiencer of "doership" and such,
Could be the ostensible meaning of the word "you."

26

देहाहन्तेन्द्रियाणां साक्षी तेभ्यो विलक्षणत्वेन ।
प्रतिभाति योऽवबोधः प्रोक्तोऽसौ त्वंपदस्य लक्ष्योऽर्थः ॥ २६ ॥

deh-āhant-endriyāṇāṁ sākṣī tebhyo vilakṣaṇatvena
pratibhāti yo'vabodhaḥ prokto'sau tvaṁ-padasya
lakṣyo'rthaḥ

deha-ahanta-indriyanam **of the body, ego, and senses** saksi **witness** tebhyah **from them** vilaksanatvena **being distinct** pratibhati yah **that which shines** avabodhah **knowledge** proktah **is said to be** asau **this** tvam padasya **of the word "you"** laksyah-arthah **the denoted meaning**

The witness that shines distinct
From the body, ego, and senses—
The knowledge of this is said to be
The denoted meaning of the word "you."

27

वेदावसानवाचा संवेद्यं सकलजगदुपादानम् ।
सर्वज्ञताद्युपेतं चैतन्यं तत्पदस्य वाच्योऽर्थः ॥ २७ ॥

vedāvasāna-vācā saṁvedyaṁ sakala-jagad-upādānam
sarvajñatādy-upetaṁ caitanyaṁ tat-padasya
vācyo'rthaḥ

veda-avasana-vacasa **by the words of the Vedic conclusions** samvedyam **to be known** sakala-jagat **of the entire manifest universe** upadanam **the material cause** sarvajnata-adi **omniscience and such** upetam **endowed with** caitanyam **Consciousness/Supreme Spirit** tat-padasya **of the word "That"** vacyah-arthah **the ostensible meaning**

The material cause of the entire manifest universe,
To be known by the words of the Vedic conclusions,
Endowed with omniscience and such—
Consciousness is the ostensible meaning of the word
"That."

28

विविधोपाधिविमुक्तं विश्वातीतं विशुद्धमद्वैतम् ।
अक्षरमनुभववेद्यं चैतन्यं तत्पदस्य लक्ष्योऽर्थः ॥ २८ ॥

vividhopādhi-vimuktaṁ viśvātītaṁ viśuddham-
advaitam
akṣaram-anubhava-vedyaṁ caitanyaṁ tat-padasya
lakṣyo'rthaḥ

vividha-upadhi-vimuktam **free of various condition-ings** visva-atitam **transcending the universe** visuddham **immaculate** advaitam **without a second** aksaram **decayless** anubhava-vedyam **to be cognized by (direct) experience** caitanyam **Consciousness/ Supreme Spirit** tat-padasya **of the word "That"** laksyah-arthah **the denoted meaning**

Free of various conditionings, transcending the
universe,
Immaculate, without a second, decayless,
To be cognized by (direct) experience—
Consciousness is the denoted meaning of the word
"That."

29

सामानाधिकरण्यं तदनु विशेषणविशेष्यता चेति ।

अथ लक्ष्यलक्षकत्वं भवति पदार्थात्मनां च संबन्धः ॥२९ ॥

sāmānādhikaraṇyaṁ tadanu viśeṣaṇa-viśeṣyatā ceti
atha lakṣya-lakṣakatvaṁ bhavati padārth-ātmanāṁ ca
saṁbandhaḥ

samana-adhikaranyam **being of the same category** tad-anu **thereafter** visesana-visesyata **the attribute and the object** ca-iti **and thus** atha **then** laksya-laksakatvam **the denoted and the apparent** bhavati **becomes** pada-artha **the words and the meaning** atmanam ca **and to each other** sambandhah **connection**

Being of the same category
Or as the attribute and the object (qualified)
Or as the apparent and the denoted,
Such are the words and meaning and their mutual
connection.

30

एकत्र वृत्तिरर्थे शब्दानां भिन्नवृत्तिहेतूनाम् ।
सामानाधिकरण्यं भवतीत्येवं वदन्ति लाक्षणिकाः ॥ ३० ॥

ekatra vṛttir-arthe śabdānāṁ bhinna-vṛtti-hetūnām
sāmānādhikaraṇyaṁ bhavatīty-evaṁ vadanti
lākṣaṇikāḥ

ekatra vrttih **similarity of mode** arthe sabdanam **in interpreting words** bhinna-vrtti-hetunam **which admit of diverse modes** samana-adhikaranyam **bringing into the same category** bhavati **is** iti-evam **in this manner** vadanti **say** laksanikah **those versed in interpretation**

Interpreting words admitting of diverse modes
To be in a similar mode
Is "bringing into the same category"—
Thus say those versed in interpretation.

31

प्रत्यक्ष्यं परोक्षयं परिपूर्णत्वं च सद्वितीयत्वम् ।

इतरेतरं विरुद्धं तत इह भवितव्यमेव लक्षणया ॥ ३१ ॥

prātyakṣyaṁ pārokṣyaṁ paripūrṇatvaṁ ca sa-
dvitīyatvam
itaretaraṁ viruddhaṁ tata iha bhavitavyam-eva
lakṣaṇayā

pratyaksyam **immediate visibility** paroksyam **invisibility** paripuranatvam **Absolute perfection** ca **and** sa-dvitiyatvam **being with a second** itara-itaram viruddham **are contradictory to one another** tatah **therefore** iha **here** bhavitavyam **there should be** eva laksanaya **only by the denoted meaning**

Immediate visibility, invisibility,
Absolute Perfection and being with a second,
Are mutually contradictory—
Hence there should be only the denoted meaning.

32

मानान्तरोपरोधे मुख्यार्थस्यापरिग्रहे जाते ।
मुख्याविनाकृतेऽर्थे या वृत्तिः सैव लक्षणा प्रोक्ता ॥ ३२ ॥

mānāntar-oparodhe mukhyārthasy-āparigrahe jāte
mukhyā-vinā-kṛte'rthe yā vṛttiḥ saiva lakṣaṇā proktā

mana-antara **due to other methods/reasons/means of proof** uparodhe **proving an obstacle** mukhya-arthasya **the primary meaning** aparigrahe jate **becoming unacceptable** mukhya-avina-krte-arthe **intended for not nullifying the primary sense** yah vrttih **that which is the mode** sa-eva **that indeed** laksana-prokta **is said to be the denoted meaning**

Where the primary meaning becomes unacceptable
Due to other reasons proving to be an obstacle,
The mode which is intended for not nullifying the primary meaning
Is indeed said to be the denoted meaning.

33

निखिलमपि वाच्यमर्थं त्यक्त्वा वृत्तिस्तदन्वितेऽन्यार्थे।
जहतीति लक्षणा स्याद्गङ्गायां घोष इतिवदत्र न ग्राह्या ॥ ३३ ॥

nikhilam-api vācyam-arthaṁ-tyaktva vṛttis-tad-
anvite'nyārthe
jahatīti lakṣaṇā syād-gaṅgāyāṁ ghoṣa iti-vad-atra na
grāhyā

nikhilam-api **totally all** vacyam-artham **ostensible (apparent) meaning** tyaktva **discarding** vrttih **the mode** tad-anvite **when it is attended by** anya-arthe **a different meaning** jahati-iti laksana-syat **will be the jahat-laksana** gangayam gosah **"the hamlet/cowherd station on the Ganga"** iti-vat **like these** atra **here** na grahya **should not be adopted**

The mode which discards all ostensible meanings
And is attended by a different meaning,
As in "the hamlet on the Ganges," will be the jahat-laksana,
And such should not be adopted here.

34

वाच्यार्थमत्यजन्त्या यस्या वृत्तेः प्रवृत्तिरन्यार्थे ।

इयमजहतीति कथिता शोणो धावतिवदत्र न ग्राह्या ॥ ३४ ॥

vācyārtham-atyajantyā yasyā vṛtteḥ pravṛttir-anyārthe
iyam-ajahatīti kathitā śoṇo dhāvati-vad-atra na grāhyā

vacyartham **the apparent meaning** a-tyajantya **without discarding** yasya vrtteh **of which mode** pravrttih **application** anyarthe **to another object** iyam **this** ajahati-iti kathita **is said to be ajahat (laksana)** sonah-dhavati-vat **like "the red runs"** atra **here** na grahya **should not be adopted**

The mode (of interpretation) which applies to another object,
Without discarding the apparent meaning—as in "the red runs,"
Is said to be the ajahat (laksana)
And should not be adopted here.

35

जहदजहतीति सा स्याद्या वाच्यार्थैकदेशमपहाय ।
बोधयति चैकदेशं सोऽयं द्विज इतिवदाश्रयेदेनाम् ॥ ३५ ॥

jahad-ajahatīti sā syād-yā vācyārth-aikadeśam-apahāya
bodhayati caikadeśaṁ so'yaṁ dvija iti-vad-āśrayed-enām

jahad-ajahad-iti sa **as jahat-ajahat** syat **is** ya **that which** vacyarthah **the ostensible meaning** ekadesam **in part** apahaya **excluding** bodhayati ca **and denotes** ekadesam **a part** sah-ayam dvijah **"He is this brahmin"** iti-vad **in this manner** asrayet **should be adopted** enam **in this case**

Jahat-ajahat is that which
Excludes in part the ostensible meaning,
And denotes a part—as in "He is this brahmin."
This mode should be adopted in this case.

36

सोऽयं द्विज इति वाक्यं त्यक्त्वा प्रत्यक्परोक्षदेशाद्यम् ।
द्विजमात्रलक्षकत्वात्कथयत्यैक्यं पदार्थयोरुभयोः ॥ ३६ ॥

so'yaṁ dvija iti vākyaṁ tyaktvā pratyak-parokṣa-
deśādyam
dvija-mātra-lakṣakatvāt-kathayaty-aikyaṁ
padārthayor-ubhayoḥ

sah-ayam dvijah **"He is this brahmin"** iti vakyam **this sentence** tyaktva **discarding** pratyak-paroksa-desa-adyam **the immediacy, invisibility of the places and such** dvija-matra **brahmin alone** laksakatvat **characteristic** kathayati **expresses** aikyam **identity** pada-arthayoh-ubhayoh **of the two word meanings**

The sentence, "He is this brahmin,"
Discarding the immediacy and invisibility of the
places and such,
Denoting only the characteristic of "brahmin,"
Expresses the identity of the two word meanings.

37

तद्वत्तत्त्वमसीति त्यक्त्वा प्रत्यक्परोक्षतादीनि ।

चिद्वस्तु लक्षयित्वा बोधयति स्पष्टमसिपदेनैक्यम् ॥ ३७ ॥

tadvat-tat-tvam-asīti tyaktvā pratyak-parokṣat-ādīni
cid-vastu lakṣayitvā bodhayati spaṣṭam-asi-paden-
aikyam

tad-vat **in the same way** tat-tvam-asi-iti **"That you are" and such** tyaktva **discarding** pratyak **immediacy** paroksata-adini **invisibility and such** cid-vastu **the thing Consciousness** laksayitva **making it the aim** bodhayati **expresses** spastam **clearly** asi-padena **by the word "are"** aikyam **identity**

Likewise, "That you are" and such,
Discarding immediacy and invisibility and such,
And making Consciousness the thing aimed at,
Express clearly by the word, "are," the identity.

38

इत्थं बोधितमर्थं महता वाक्येन दर्शितैक्येन ।
अहमित्यपरोक्षयतां वेदो वेदयति वीतशोकत्वम् ॥ ३८ ॥

ittham̐ bodhitam-artham̐ mahatā vākyena darśit-
aikyena
aham-ityaparokṣayatām̐ vedo vedayati vīta-śokatvam

ittham **in this way** bodhitam-artham **the meaning expressed** mahata vakyena **by the great aphorism (profound saying)** darsita **showing** aikyena **identity** aham iti **that this is I** aparoksayatam **to those who have direct awareness** vedah **the Veda-s** vedayati **makes known/declares** vitasokatvam **freedom from sorrow**

The meaning expressed by the great aphorism
Showing identity in this way—that this is I—
For those who have this direct Awareness,
The Veda-s declare freedom from sorrow.

39

प्रायः प्रवर्तकत्वं विधिवचसां लोकवेदयोर्दृष्टम् ।
सिद्धं बोधयतोऽर्थं कथमिव तद्भवति तत्त्वमस्यादेः ॥ ३९ ॥

prāyaḥ pravartakatvaṁ vidhi-vacasāṁ loka-vedayor-dṛṣṭam
siddhaṁ bodhayato'rthaṁ katham-iva tad-bhavati tat-tvam-asyādeḥ

prayah **mostly** pravartakatvam **call to action** vidhi-vacasam **of words of injunction** loka-vedayoh **of worldly and Vedic** drstam **is seen** siddham **a con clusion** bodhayatah **expressing** artham **meaning** katham-iva **how indeed** tat-bhavati **that is/that becomes** tat-tvamasi-adeh **"That you are" and such**

Mostly, a call to action is seen
In words of injunction, worldly and Vedic.
How, indeed, can a meaning expressing a conclusion
Such as "That you are" become one (an injunction)?

40

विधिरेव न प्रवृत्तिं जनयत्यभिलषितवस्तुबोधोऽपि ।
राजा याति सुतोऽभूदिति बोधेन प्रवर्तते लोकः ॥ ४० ॥

vidhir-eva na pravṛttiṁ janayaty-abhilaṣita-vastu-
bodho'pi
rājā yāti suto'bhūd-iti bodhena pravartate lokaḥ

vidhih-eva **injunction alone** na pravrttim janayati **does not generate action** abhilasita-vastu **desired object** bodhah-api **Knowledge also** raja yati **the king goes** sutah-abhuta **son has been born** iti bodhena **by such knowledge** pravartate **goes into, action** lokah **people**

Injunction alone does not generate action;
Knowledge of desired objects can also do so.
People commence activity
By knowledge such as "the king goes," [or] "a son has been born."

41

ऐक्यपरैः श्रुतिवाक्यैरात्मा शश्वत्प्रकाश्यमानोऽपि ।
देशिकदयाविहीनैरपरोक्षयितुं न शक्यते पुरुषैः ॥ ४१ ॥

aikya-paraiḥ śruti-vākyair-ātmā śaśvat-prakāśya-
mano'pi
deśika-dayā-vihīnair-aparokṣayituṁ na śakyate
puruṣaiḥ

aikya-paraih **declaring identity** sruti-vakyaih **according to the words of the Veda-s/by the Veda-s** atma **the Self** sasvat **eternally** prakasyamanah-api **even though illumines** desika-daya-vihinaih **by those devoid of the Grace of the Master** aparoksayitum **to have direct Awareness** na sakyate **is not possible** purusaih **for people**

Though the Self eternally illumines,
According to the words of the Veda-s declaring identity,
For people devoid of the Grace of the Master,
It is not possible to have direct Awareness.

42

विरहितकाम्यनिषिद्धो विहितानुष्ठाननिर्मलस्वान्तः ।
भजति निजमेव बोधं गुरुणा किमिति त्वया न मन्तव्यम् ॥४२ ॥

virahita-kāmya-niṣiddho vihit-ānuṣṭhāna-nirmala-
svāntaḥ
bhajati nijam-eva bodhaṁ guruṇā kim-iti tvayā na
mantavyam

virahita-kamya **avoiding rites** nisiddhah **prohibited** vihita-anusthana **practising the prescribed** nirmala **pure, stainless** svantah **in one's mind** bhajati **attains** nijam-eva **by oneself** bodham **knowledge** guruna kim **why, the Guru?** iti **thus** tvaya **by you** na mantavyam **should not be thought of**

"Avoiding prohibited rites, practicing the prescribed
[rites],
And stainless in one's mind,
One attains knowledge by oneself;
[So,] why the Guru?"—you should not think thus.

43

कर्मभिरेव न बोधः प्रभवति गुरुणा विना दयानिधिना ।
आचार्यवान्हि पुरुषो वेदेत्यर्थस्य वेदसिद्धत्वात् ॥४३ ॥

karmabhir-eva na bodhaḥ prabhavati guruṇā vinā
daya̅-nidhinā
ācāryavān-hi puruṣo vedety-arthasya veda-siddhatvāt

karmabhih eva **by rites alone** bodham **Knowledge** na prabhavati **does not arise** guruna-vina **without a Guru** daya-nidhina **the abode of compassion** acaryavan-hi **only one with a Teacher** purusah **person** veda-iti **can know, thus** arthasya **meaning** veda-siddhatvat **being the conclusion of the Veda-s**

By rites alone, Knowledge does not arise,
Without a Guru, the abode of compassion.
Only one with a Teacher can know—
Thus is the conclusion of the meaning of the Veda-s.

44

वेदोऽनादितया वा यद्वा परमेश्वरप्रणीततया ।

भवति परमं प्रमाणं बोधो नास्ति स्वतश्च परतो वा ॥ ४४ ॥

vedo'nāditayā vā yadvā parameśvara-praṇītatayā
bhavati paramaṁ pramāṇaṁ bodho nāsti svataśca
parato vā

vedah **the Veda-s** anadi-taya va **either because of being beginningless** yad-va **or because of** paramesvara-pranita-taya **being delivered by the Supreme Lord** bhavati **becomes** paramam pramanam **the highest authority** bodhah **Knowledge** na-asti **is not** svatah-ca **on its own and** paratah-va **or from other (authorities)**

The Veda-s, either because of being beginningless
Or because of being pronouncements of the Supreme Lord,
Become the highest standard of authority;
Knowledge does not arise on its own, or from others (authorities).

45

नापेक्षते यदन्यद्यदपेक्षन्तेऽखिलानि मानानि ।
वाक्यं तन्निगमानां मानं ब्रह्माद्यतीन्द्रियावगतौ ॥ ४५ ॥

nā-pekṣate yad-anyad-yad-apekṣante'khilāni mānāni
vākyaṁ tan-nigamānāṁ mānaṁ brahmādy-atīndriy-
āvagatau

na-apeksate yat **that which does not depend upon** anyat **anything else** yat-apeksante-akhilani manani **which all proofs depend upon** vakyam tat-nigamanam **that sentence of the Veda-s** manam **is the proof** brahma-adi **of Brahman and others** ati-indriya-avagatau **in the comprehension transcending the senses**

That which does not depend upon anything else,
Upon which all proofs depend,
That sentence of the Veda-s is the proof
In the comprehension of Brahman and others
transcending the senses.

46

मानं प्रबोधयन्तं बोधं मानेन ये बुभुत्सन्ते ।

एधोभिरेव दहनं दग्धुं वाञ्छन्ति ते महात्मानः ॥४६ ॥

mānaṁ prabodhayantaṁ bodhaṁ mānena ye
bubhutsante
edhobhir-eva dahanaṁ dagdhuṁ vāñchanti te
mahātmānaḥ

manam prabodhayantam **giving rise to proof** bodham **Knowledge** manena **by means of the proof** ye **(those) who** bubhutsante **strive** edhobhih-eva **by means of fuel itself** dahanam **fire** dagdhum **to burn** vanchanti **desire** te mahatmanah **those great ones**

Those who strive by means of a proof
To attain Knowledge, which gives rise to such proof,
Are indeed "great ones"
Who desire to burn fire by means of fuel itself.

47

वेदोऽनादिरमुष्य व्यञ्जक ईशः स्वयंप्रकाशात्मा ।
तदभिव्यक्तिमुदीक्ष्य प्रोक्तोऽसौ सूरिभिः प्रमाणमिति ॥ ४७ ॥

vedo'nādir-amuṣya vyañjaka īśaḥ svayaṁ-prakāśātmā
tad-abhivyaktim-udīkṣya prokto'sau sūribhiḥ
pramāṇam-iti

vedah **the Veda-s** anadih **are beginningless** amusya-vyanjakah **the one who makes this clear** isah **is Isvara/is the Lord** svayam-prakasa-atma **the self-luminous Atma** tad-abhivyaktim **the manifestation of this** udiksya **keeping in view** proktah **it has been said** asau **this** suribhih **by the great ones** pramanam-iti **that it is the authority**

The Veda-s are beginningless,
And the One who makes this clear is Isvara (the Lord), the self-luminous Atma (the Self).
Keeping in view the manifestation of this (by Isvara)
It has been said by the great ones that they (the Veda-s) are the highest authority.

48

रूपाणामवलोके चक्षुरिवान्यन्न कारणं दृष्टम् ।
तद्वददृष्टावगतौ वेदवदन्यो न वेदको हेतुः ॥ ४८ ॥

rūpāṇām-avaloke cakṣur-ivānyan-na kāraṇaṁ dṛṣṭam
tadvad-adṛṣṭ-āvagatau vedavad-anyo na vedako hetuḥ

rupanam **of forms** avaloke **in seeing** caksuh-iva **like the eye** anyat **another** na karanam **not a cause** drstam **is seen** tad-vat **like that** adrsta-avagatau **in realizing the unseen** veda-vat **equal to the Veda-s** anyah **another** na vedako hetuh **for making known not the cause**

In seeing forms, no other cause than the eye is seen.
Like that, in realizing the unseen,
No other cause equal to the Veda-s
Can make us know.

49

निगमेषु निश्चितार्थं तन्त्रे कश्चिद्यदि प्रकाशयति ।

तदिदमनुवादमात्रं प्रामाण्यं तस्य सिध्यति न किंचित् ॥ ४९ ॥

nigameṣu niścitārthaṁ tantre kaścid-yadi prakāśayati
tad-idam-anuvāda-mātraṁ prāmāṇyaṁ tasya sidhyati
na kiñcit

nigamesu **in the Veda-s** niscita **established** artham **meaning** tantre-kascid **in some treatises** yadi **if** prakasayati **is shown** tat **that** idam **this** anuvada-matram **is merely an explanatory repetition** pramanyam **authority** tasya sidhyati na **it does not attain** kincit **even a little**

If the meaning established in the Veda-s
Is shown in some treatises,
Such is merely an explanatory repetition
And does not become an authority in the least.

50

अंशद्वयवति निगमे साधयति द्वैतमेव कोऽप्यंशः ।
अद्वैतमेव वस्तु प्रतिपादयति प्रसिद्धमपरोंऽशः ॥ ५० ॥

aṁśa-dvaya-vati nigame sādhayati dvaitam-eva ko'pyaṁśaḥ
advaitam-eva vastu pratipādayati prasiddham-aparo'ṁśaḥ

amsa-dvaya-vati **having two parts** nigame **in the Veda-s** sadhayati **establishes** dvaitam-eva **only the dual** kah-api-amsah **some portion** advaitam-eva **only the nondual** vastu **thing/substance/the real** pratipadayati **expounds** prasiddham **well known** aparah-amsah **the other part**

Of the Veda-s, having two parts, some portion
Establishes only the dual,
And another well known part
Expounds only the nondual, real thing.

51

अद्वैतमेव सत्यं तस्मिन्द्वैतं न सत्यमध्यस्तम् ।
रजतमिव शुक्तिकायां मृगतृष्णायामिवोदकस्फुरणम् ॥ ५१ ॥

advaitam-eva satyaṁ tasmin-dvaitaṁ na satyam-
adhyastam
rajatam-iva śuktikāyāṁ mṛga-tṛṣṇāyām-ivodaka-
sphuraṇam

advaitam-eva **the nondual alone** satyam **is the Truth** tasmin **in that** dvaitam **the dual** na satyam **is not the Truth** adhyastam **it is superimposed** rajatam-iva **like silver** suktikayam **on mother-of-pearl** mrga-trsnayam-iva **as in a mirage** udaka-sphuranam **the shimmering of water**

The nondual alone is the Truth;
The dual, superimposed on the Truth, is not the
Truth.
[It is] like silver on the mother-of-pearl
And as the shimmering of water in a mirage.

52

आरोपितं यदि स्यादद्वैतं वस्त्ववस्तुनि द्वैते ।
तदयुक्तमेव यस्मात्सत्येऽध्यासो भवत्यसत्यानाम् ॥ ५२ ॥

āropitaṁ yadi syād-advaitaṁ vastv-avastuni dvaite
tad-ayuktam-eva yasmāt-satye'dhyāso bhavaty-
asatyānām

aropitam **superimposition** yadi syat **if there be** advaitam vastu **nondual entity** avastuni dvaite **on the unreal and dual thing** tat **that** ayuktam-eva **is not possible at all** yasmat **because** satye **on the real** adhyasah **superimposition** bhavati **is/becomes** asatyanam **of the unreal**

If there be (the thought of) "superimposition
Of the nondual on the unreal and dual,"
It is not possible at all, because
Superimposition is of the unreal on the real.

53

यद्यारोपणमुभयोस्तद्व्यतिरिक्तस्य कस्यचिदभावात् ।
आरोपणं न शून्ये तस्माददद्वैतसत्यता ग्राह्या ॥ ५३ ॥

yady-āropaṇam-ubhayos-tad-vyatiriktasya kasyacid-
abhāvāt
āropaṇaṁ na śūnye tasmād-advaita-satyatā grāhyā

yadi **if there be** aropanam **superimposition** ubhayoh **of both** tat-vyatiriktasya **different from that** kasyacit **anything else at all** abhavat **being non-existent** aropanam **superimposition** na sunye **not on nothing** tasmat **hence** advaita-satyah **the truthfulness of the nondual** grahya **should be accepted**

If there be superimposition of both,
There being no difference of one from the other,*
Superimposition cannot be on nothing;
Hence, the truthfulness of the nondual should be accepted.

*Alt. trans.: Anything else at all different therefrom being nonexistent,

54

प्रत्यक्षाद्यनवगतं श्रुत्या प्रतिपादनीयमद्वैतम् ।
द्वैतं न प्रतिपाद्यं तस्य स्वत एव लोकसिद्धत्वात् ॥ ५४ ॥

pratyakṣādy-anavagataṁ śrutyā pratipādanīyam-
advaitam
dvaitaṁ na pratipādyaṁ tasya svata eva loka-
siddhatvāt

pratyaksa-adi **by immediate perception and such** anavagatam **not understood** srutya **by the Veda-s** pratipadaniyam **is to be establised** advaitam **Non-duality** dvaitam **duality** na pratipadyam **(does) not (need) to be established** tasya **of it** svata eva **on its own** loka-siddhatvat **being concluded by worldly means**

Nonduality, not understood by immediate perception and such,
Is to be established by the Veda-s.
Duality does not need to be established,
It being concluded, on its own, by worldly means.

55

अद्वैतं सुखरूपं दुःसह दुःखं सदा भवेद्द्वैतम् ।
यत्र प्रयोजनं स्यात्प्रतिपादयति श्रुतिस्तदेवासौ ॥ ५५ ॥

advaitaṁ sukha-rūpaṁ duḥsaha duḥkhaṁ sadā
bhaved-dvaitam
yatra prayojanaṁ syāt-pratipādayati śrutis-tadevāsau

advaitam **Nonduality** sukha-rupam **is of the nature of happiness** duhsaha duhkham **intolerable sorrow** sada **always** bhavet **will be** dvaitam **duality** yatra **where** prayojanam syat **there is a purpose** pratipadayati **establishes** srutih **the Veda-s** tat-eva **that indeed** asau **is this**

Nonduality is of the nature of happiness.
Duality will always be intolerable sorrow.
The Veda-s establish what is purposeful:
"That, indeed, is this."

56

निगमगिरा प्रतिपाद्यं वस्तु यदानन्दरूपमद्वैतम् ।
स्वाभाविकं स्वरूपं जीवत्वं तस्य केचन ब्रुवते ॥ ५६ ॥

nigama-girā pratipādyaṁ vastu yad-ānanda-rūpam-advaitam
svābhāvikaṁ svarūpaṁ jīvatvaṁ tasya kecana bruvate

nigama-gira **by the words of the Veda-s** pratipadyam **what is established** vastu **a thing/real substance** yat **which** ananda-rupam **of the nature of bliss** advaitam **nondual** svabhavikam **one's own nature/natural/inherent** svarupam **nature** jivatvam **jiva-hood, individual self-hood** tasya **of it** kecana **some** bruvate **say**

What is established by the word of the Veda-s—
A real thing that is nondual
And of the nature of bliss—
"Its inherent nature is jiva-hood (individuality),"
some say.

57

स्वाभाविकं यदि स्याज्जीवत्वं तस्य विशदविज्ञप्तेः ।

सकृदपि न तद्विनाशं गच्छेदुष्णप्रकाशवद्वह्नेः ॥ ५७ ॥

svābhāvikaṁ yadi syāj-jīvatvaṁ tasya viśada-vijñapteḥ
sakṛd-api na tad-vināśam gacched-uṣṇa-prakāśa-vad-
vahneḥ

svabhavikam **own nature/ inherent** yadi syat **if be** jivatvam **jiva-hood** tasya **of that** visada-vijnapteh **revered as the shining/bright/conspicuous/brilliant** sakrd-api **even once, for a moment,** na tad-vinasam-gacchet **it will not get destroyed** usna-prakasa-vat **like heat and light** vahneh **of fire**

If the inherent nature of that revered
As the brilliant be jiva-hood (individuality),
It (individuality, jiva-hood) will not get destroyed
even for a moment,
Like the heat and light of fire.

58

यद्वदयो रसविद्धं काञ्चनतां याति तद्वदेवासौ ।
जीवः साधनशक्त्या परतां यातीति केचिदिच्छन्ति ॥ ५८ ॥

yad-vad-ayo rasa-viddhaṁ kāñcanatāṁ yāti tadvad-
evāsau
jīvaḥ sādhana-śaktyā paratāṁ yātīti kecid-icchanti

yad-vat **just as** ayah **iron** rasa-viddham **acted upon by some chemical** kancanatam **golden-ness** yati **attains** tadvat **likewise** eva **indeed** asau jivah **this jiva** sadhana-saktya **by the power of spiritual effort** paratam **the Supreme State** yati **attains** iti **thus** kecit **some** icchanti **opine**

Just as iron becomes golden
[When] acted upon by some chemical,
Likewise this jiva (individual), by the power of
spiritual effort,
Attains the Supreme State—so opine some.

59

तदिदं भवति न युक्तं गतवति तस्मिंश्चिरेण रसवीर्ये ।
प्रतिपद्यते प्रणाशं हैमो वर्णोऽप्ययः समारूढः ॥ ५९ ॥

tad-idaṁ bhavati na yuktaṁ gatavati tasmiṁś-cireṇa
rasa-vīrye
pratipadyate praṇāśaṁ haimo varṇo'pyayaḥ
samārūḍhaḥ

tat **that** idam **this** bhavati **becomes** na yuktam **is not correct** gatavati **when there passes away** tasmin **in it** cirena **after a lapse of time** rasa-virye **the power of the chemical** pratipadyate **reaches** pranasam **destruction** hemau **in the golden** varnah-api **color also** ayah samarudhah **on the iron**

It is not correct that this (jiva, individual) becomes
That (Supreme);
As the power of the chemical
Passes away after a lapse of time,
So does the golden color on the iron reach
destruction.

60

जीवत्वमपि तथेदं बहुविधसुखदुःखलक्षणोपेतम् ।
गतमिव साधनशक्त्या प्रतिभात्येव प्रयाति न विनाशम् ॥ ६० ॥

jīvatvam-api tathedaṁ bahu-vidha-sukha-duḥkha-
lakṣaṇopetam
gatam-iva sādhana-śaktyā pratibhāty-eva prayāti na
vināśam

jivatvam-api **jiva-hood (individuality) also** tatha **likewise** idam **this** bahu-vidha **variegated** sukha **happiness** duhkha **sorrow** laksana-upetam **endowed with characteristics** gatam-iva **as if has reached** sadhana-saktya **by the power of effort/production** pratibhati eva **only appear** prayati **reaches** na vinasam **no destruction**

Likewise, endowed with variegated characteristics of
happiness and sorrow,
This jiva-hood (individuality), also, would only
appear
As if it had reached [the state of being the Supreme],
by the power of effort,
But [its nature] will not be destroyed.

61

तस्मात्स्वतो यदि स्याज्जीवः सततं स एव जीवः स्यात् ।
एवं यदि परमात्मा परमात्मैवायमिति भवेद्युक्तम् ॥ ६१ ॥

tasmāt-svato yadi syāj-jīvaḥ satataṁ sa eva jīvaḥ syāt
evaṁ yadi paramātmā paramātmaiv-āyam-iti bhaved-
yuktam

tasmat **hence** svatah **by its nature** yadi syat-jivah **if it be jiva** satatam **always** sa eva **that itself** jivah syat **will be jiva** evam yadi **if thus** paramatma **it is the Supreme Self** paramatma-eva **only the Supreme Self** ayam iti **this thus** bhaved **will be** yuktam **correct**

Hence, if it be jiva (the individual) by its nature,
It will always thus be jiva itself.
If it is the Supreme Self, it will thus be
Only the Supreme Self—this will be the right
conclusion.

62

यदि वा परेण साम्यं जीवश्चेद्भजति साधनबलेन ।
कालेन तदपि कियता नश्यत्येवेति निश्चितं सकलैः ॥ ६२ ॥

yadi vā pareṇa sāmyaṁ jīvaś-ced-bhajati sādhana-
balena
kālena tadapi kiyatā naśyaty-eveti niścitaṁ sakalaiḥ

yadi va **even if** parena samyam **similarity with the Supreme** jivah-cet **if the jiva** bhajati **attains** sadhana-balena **by the strength of effort** kalena **with the lapse of time** tadapi **even that** kiyata **however much** nasyati-eva **indeed perishes** iti **thus** niscitam **it has been decided** sakalaih **by all**

Even if the jiva (individual) attains, by the
strength of effort,
Similarity with the Supreme,
Even that, however much, indeed perishes
With the lapse of time—thus it has been decided
by all.

63

तस्मात्परं स्वकीयं देहं मोहात्मकं च संसारम् ।
स्वज्ञानेन ग्रसित्वा पूर्णः स्वयमेव शिष्यते नान्यत् ॥ ६३ ॥

tasmāt-paraṁ svakīyaṁ dehaṁ mohātmakaṁ ca
saṁsāram
sva-jñānena grasitvā pūrṇaḥ svayam-eva śiṣyate
nānyat

tasmat **therefore** param **the great** svakiyam deham **one's own body** moha-atmakam **filled with delusion** ca samsaram **and the birth-death cycle** sva-jnanena **by one's own Knowledge** grasitva **destroying** purnah **the perfect** svayam-eva **by oneself** sisyate **remains** na-anyat **there remains nothing else**

Therefore, destroying, by one's own Knowledge,
One's own body and the great delusion-filled
samsara (repetitive cycle of birth and death),
One remains by oneself, the Perfect,
And nothing else remains.

64

सत्यं ज्ञानमनन्तं प्रकृतं परमात्मरूपमद्वैतम् ।
अवबोधयन्ति निखिलाः श्रुतयः स्मृतिभिः समं समस्ताभिः ॥ ६४ ॥

satyaṁ jñānam-anantaṁ prakṛtaṁ paramātma-rūpam-advaitam
avabodhayanti nikhilāḥ śrutayaḥ smṛtibhiḥ samaṁ samastābhiḥ

satyam jnanam-anantam **Being, Knowledge and Infinity** prakrtam **the subject under discussion** paramatma-rupam **is the nature of the Supreme Self** advaitam **nondual** avabodhayanti **expound** nikhilah **all** srutayah **the Veda-s** smrtibhih samam **along with the recollected treatises** samastabhih **with all of them**

All the Veda-s, along with all treatises of recollection,
Expound the subject under discussion:
The nature of the nondual Supreme Self,
As Being-Knowledge-Infinity.

65

अद्वैतबोधकानां निखिलानां निगमवाक्यजालानाम् ।
वाक्यान्तराणि सकलान्यभिधीयन्तेऽस्य शेषभूतानि ॥ ६५ ॥

advaita-bodhakānāṁ nikhilānāṁ nigama-vākya-
jālānām
vākyāntarāṇi sakalāny-abhidhīyante'sya śeṣa-bhūtāni

advaita-bodhakanam **teaching the nondual** nikhilanam **to all** nigama-vakya-jalanam **passages of Vedic words** vakya-antarani **other words** sakalani **all** abhidiyante **denote** asya **of this** sesa-bhutani **those that remain**

In regard to all the passages of Vedic words
Teaching Nonduality,
All other remaining passages
Denote the same.

66

यस्मिन्मिहिरवदुदिते तिमिरवदपयान्ति कर्तृतादीनि ।
ज्ञानं विरहितभेदं कथमिव तद्भवति तत्त्वमस्यादेः ॥ ६६ ॥

yasmin-mihiravad-udite timira-vad-apayānti kartṛt-
ādīni
jñānaṁ virahita-bhedaṁ katham-iva tad-bhavati
tattvamasy-ādeḥ

yasmin **wherein** mihira-vat **like the sun** udite **on rising** timira-vat **like darkness** apayanti **go away/disappear** kartrta-adini **doership and such**
jnanam **Knowledge** virahita-bhedam **without differences** katham-iva **how indeed** tat **that** bhavati **arises/becomes** tat-tvam-asi-adeh **of "That you are" and such**

Wherein, like darkness upon the sun rising,
Disappear doership and such—
How, indeed, does that Knowledge of "That you are"
and such,
Without differences, come to be?

67

कर्मप्रकरणनिष्ठं ज्ञानं कर्माङ्गमिष्यते प्राज्ञैः ।
भिन्नप्रकरणभाजः कर्माङ्गत्वं कथं भवेज्ज्ञप्तेः ॥ ६७ ॥

karma-prakaraṇa-niṣṭhaṁ jñānaṁ karmāṅgam-iṣyate prājñaiḥ
bhinna-prakaraṇa-bhājaḥ karmāṅgatvaṁ kathaṁ bhavej-jñapteḥ

karma-prakarana-nistham **placed in the ritual section** jnanam **knowledge** karma-angam **part/limb/division of rituals** isyate **is said to be** prajnaih **by the wise** bhinna-prakarana **different section** bhajah **praising** karma-angamtvam **the portion of rituals/state of subordination to action/ ritual** katham **how** bhavet **becomes** jnapteh **of Knowledge**

Placed in the rituals section (of the Veda-s)
Is the knowledge about (various) parts of rituals—so say the wise.
How can the portion of rituals extolled in a different section
Become (the section of) Knowledge?*

*Alt. trans.: How can Knowledge be subordinate to ritual, since it occurs in a different context?

68

अधिकारिविषयभेदौ कर्मज्ञानात्मकावुभौ काण्डौ ।
एवं सति कथमनयोरङ्गाङ्गित्वं परस्परं घटते ॥ ६८ ॥

adhikāri-viṣaya-bhedau karma-jñān-ātmakāv-ubhau
kāṇḍau
evaṁ sati katham-anayor-aṅgāṅgitvaṁ parasparaṁ
ghaṭate

adhikari **the fit person/the qualified** visaya **subject matter** bhedam **different** karma **rituals** jnana **Knowledge** atmakam **having in themselves** ubhau kandau **both portions** evam sati **being so** katham-anayoh **how between these** anga-angitvam **the principal and the subordinate** parasparam **mutual** ghatate **is brought about**

The qualified person and the subject matter
Contained in both portions are different.
This being so, how can mutual relationship of the
principal and the subordinate
Be brought about between rituals and Knowledge?

69

ज्ञानं कर्मणि न स्याज्ज्ञाने कर्मेदमपि तथा न स्यात् ।

तत्कथमनयोरुभयोस्तपनतमोवत्समुच्चयो घटते ॥ ६९ ॥

jñānaṁ karmaṇi na syāj-jñāne karmedam-api tathā na
syāt
tat-katham-anayor-ubhayos-tapana-tamovat-
samuccayo ghaṭate

jnanam **Knowledge** karmani **in rituals** na syat **cannot be** jnane **in Knowledge** karma **rituals** idam-api **this also** tatha **likewise** na syat **cannot be** tat **hence** katham **how** anayoh-ubhayoh **between these two** tapana-tamovat **like sun and darkness** samuccayah **conjunction** ghatate **(can) be brought about**

Knowledge cannot be in rituals;
Likewise, rituals in Knowledge also cannot be.
Hence, how can any conjunction be brought about
Between these two, which are like the sun and
darkness?

70

तस्मान्मोहनिवृत्तौ ज्ञानं न सहायमन्यदर्थयते ।
यद्वद्घनतरतिमिरप्रकरपरिध्वंसने सहस्रांशुः ॥ ७० ॥

tasmān-moha-nivṛttau jñānaṁ na sahāyam-anyad-
arthayate
yad-vad-ghanatara-timira-prakara-paridhvaṁsane
sahasrāṁśuḥ

tasmat **hence** moha-nivrttau **for warding off delusion** jnanam **Knowledge** sahayam-anyat **another help** na arthayate **does not need** yad-vat **just as** ghanatara **highly massive, very dense** timira-prakara **heap of darkness** paridhvamsane **in dispelling** sahasramsuh **the thousand-rayed sun**

Hence, for warding off delusion,
Knowledge does not need another help,
Just as the thousand-rayed sun (needs no help)
In dispelling very dense darkness.

71

ज्ञानं तदेवममलं साक्षी विश्वस्य भवति परमात्मा ।
संबध्यते न धर्मैः साक्षी तैरेव सच्चिदानन्दः ॥ ७१ ॥

jñānaṁ tad-evam-amalaṁ sākṣī viśvasya bhavati paramātmā
saṁbadhyate na dharmaiḥ sākṣī tair-eva sac-cid-ānandaḥ

jnanam **Knowledge** tat **that** evam **thus** amalam **pure/ stainless** saksi **witness** visvasya **of the universe** bhavati **is** paramatma **the Supreme Self** sambadhyate na **is not bound** dharmaih **by qualities** saksi **witness** taih **by them** eva sat-cit-anandah **verily Being-Consciousness-Bliss**

Thus, that pure, stainless Knowledge, the Supreme Self,
Is the witness of the universe,
Not bound by the qualities (of the universe),
Being the witness thereof, verily, Existence-Consciousness-Bliss.

72

रज्ज्वादेरुरगाद्यैः संबन्धवदस्य दृश्यसंबन्धः ।
सततमसङ्गोऽयमिति श्रुतिरप्यमुमर्थमेव साधयति ॥ ७२ ॥

rajjvāder-uragādyaiḥ saṁbandha-vad-asya dṛśya-
saṁbandhaḥ
satatam-asaṅgo'yam-iti śrutir-apy-amum-artham-eva
sādhayati

rajju-adeh **of the rope and such** uraga-adyaih **to the serpent and such** sambandha-vat **like the relationship** asya **of this** drsya **of the seen (the object)** sambandhah **relationship** satatam **always** asangah **is unattached** ayam **this** iti **thus** srutih-api **the Veda-s also** amum **this** artham-eva **meaning only** sadhayati **establishes**

The relationship of this to the object (the seen)
Is like the relationship of the rope and such to the
serpent and others.
The Veda-s establish this meaning only:
That this (the Self) is always unattached.

73

कर्तृ च कर्म च यस्य स्फुरति ब्रह्मैव तन्न जानाति ।
यस्य न कर्तृ न कर्म स्फुटतरमयमेव वेदितुं क्रमते ॥ ७३ ॥

kartṛ ca karma ca yasya sphurati brahmaiva tan-na jānāti
yasya na kartṛ na karma sphuṭa-taram-ayam-eva veditum kramate

kartr ca **the doer** karma ca **and the action** yasya **for whom** sphurati **appear clearly/become evident** brahma-eva **Brahman only** tat **That** na janati **[do] not know** yasya **for whom** na kartr **neither doer** na karma **nor action** sphuta-taram **very clearly** ayam-eva **this only** veditum **to know** kramate **is capable**

For whom doer and action appear clearly
Is Brahman only; these (two) do not know That.
Only That is capable of knowing
For which there is neither doer nor action.

74

कर्तृत्वादिकमेतन्मायाशक्त्या प्रपद्यते निखिलम् ।
इति केचिदाहुरेषा भ्रान्तिर्ब्रह्मातिरेकतो नान्यत् ॥ ७४ ॥

kartṛtv-ādikam-etan-māyā-śaktyā prapadyate nikhilam
iti kecid-āhur-eṣā bhrāntir-brahm-ātirekato nānyat

kartrtvadikam **doership and others** etat-maya-saktya **by its power of maya** prapadyate **displayed** nikhilam **all** iti **thus** kecid **some** ahuh **say** esah **this** bhrantih **is an error** brahma-atirekatah **different from Brahman** na-anyat **[there is] nothing else**

"Doership and others," say some,
"Are all displayed by the power of maya."
This is an error, because
There is nothing else different from Brahman.

75

तस्मिन्ब्रह्मणि विदिते विश्वमशेषं भवेदिदं विदितम् ।
कारणमृदि विदितायां घटकरकाद्या यथावगम्यन्ते ॥ ७५ ॥

tasmin-brahmaṇi vidite viśvam-aśeṣaṁ bhaved-idaṁ
viditam
kāraṇa-mṛdi viditāyāṁ ghaṭa-karakādyā
yathāvagamyante

tasmin-brahmani vidite **that Brahman being known** visvam-asesam **the entire universe** bhaved-idam **this will become** viditam **known** karana-mrdi viditayam **when clay, the cause is known** ghata-karaka-adyah **jars, water pots, and others** yatha **just as** avagamyante **become known**

That Brahman being known,
This entire universe will become known,
Just as jars, pots, and others become known
When their cause, the clay, is known.

76

तदिदं कारणमेकं विगतविशेषं विशुद्धचिद्रूपम् ।

तस्मात्सदेकरूपान्मायोपहितादभूदिदं विश्वम् ॥ ७६ ॥

tad-idaṁ kāraṇam-ekaṁ vigata-viśeṣaṁ viśuddha-cid-
rūpam
tasmāt-sad-eka-rūpān-māyopahitād-abhud-idaṁ
viśvam

tat **then** idam **this** karanam-ekam **is the one cause** vigata-visesam **without attributes** visuddha **pure** cid-rupam **of the nature of Consciousness** tasmat **therefrom** sat **the Reality** eka-rupat **the One** maya-upahitat **conditioned by maya (illusion)** abhut **came forth** idam visvam **this universe**

This, then, is the One cause, without attributes,
Of the nature of pure Consciousness.
From this, the One Reality, conditioned by maya
(illusion),
Came forth this universe.

77

कारणमसदिति केचित्कथयन्त्यसतो भवेन्न कारणता ।
अङ्कुरजननी शक्तिः सति खलु बीजे समीक्ष्यते सकलैः ॥ ७७ ॥

kāraṇam-asad-iti kecit-kathayanty-asato bhaven-na kāraṇatā
aṅkura-jananī śaktiḥ sati khalu bīje samīkṣyate sakalaiḥ

karanam **the cause** asat **unreal, nonexistent** iti **thus** kecit **some** kathayanti **say** asatah **from the unreal, nonexistent** bhavet-na **there cannot arise/become** karanata **being a cause** ankura-janani-saktih **the power to create a sprout** sati kalu bije **if the seed exists** samiksyate **is seen** sakalaih **by all**

"The cause is nonexistent," some say.
The cause cannot be of the nonexistent.
The power to create a sprout is
Only if the seed exists, as seen by all.

78

कारणमसदिति कथयन्वन्ध्यापुत्रेण निर्वहेत्कार्यम् ।
किं च मृगतृष्णिकाम्भः पीत्वोदन्यां महीयसीं शमयेत् ॥७८॥

kāraṇam-asad-iti kathayan-vandhyā-putreṇa nirvahet-
kāryam
kiṁ ca mṛga-tṛṣṇik-āmbhaḥ pītvodanyāṁ mahīyasīṁ
śamayet

karanam-asat **the cause is nonexistent** iti kathayan **saying so** vandhya-putrena **with the son of a barren woman** nirvahet **(one) should manage** karyam **affairs** kim ca **and also** mrga-trsnika **of a mirage** ambhah **waters** pitva **by drinking** udanyam mahiyasim **intense thirst** samayet **should quench**

If one says the cause is nonexistent,
One should manage affairs with the son of a barren
woman
And also quench intense thirst
By drinking the waters of a mirage.

79

यस्मान्न सोऽयमसतो वादः संभवति शास्त्रयुक्तिभ्याम् ।
तस्मात्सदेव तत्त्वं सर्वेषां भवति कारणं जगताम् ॥ ७९ ॥

yasmān-na so'yam-asato vādaḥ saṁbhavati śāstra-
yuktibhyām
tasmāt-sad-eva tattvaṁ sarveṣāṁ bhavati kāraṇaṁ
jagatām

yasmat **because of which** na sah **this (can) not** ayam **this** asatah vadah **argument of the nonexistent** sambhavati **arise** sastra-yuktibhyam **by the scriptures or by logic** tasmat **because of that** sat-eva t**he Real alone** tattvam **the Truth/Principle** sarvesam **of all** bhavati **becomes/is** karanam **the cause** jagatam **of the universe**

As this argument of the nonexistent [cause]
According to scriptures or by logic cannot be,
Therefore, the Real alone, the Truth of all,
Is the cause of the universe.

80

जगदाकारतयापि प्रथते गुरुशिष्यविग्रहतयापि ।
ब्रह्माकारतयापि प्रतिभातीदं परात्परं तत्त्वम् ॥ ८० ॥

jagad-ākāra-tayāpi prathate guru-śiṣya-vigraha-tayāpi
brahmākāra-tayāpi pratibhātīdaṁ parāt-paraṁ tattvam

jagad-akara-taya-api **in the form of the world also** prathate **manifests** guru-sisya-vigraha-taya-api **the form of Guru and disciple also** brahma-akara-taya-api **of the form of Brahma (the Creator)** pratibhati **manifests itself** idam **this** parat-param tattvam **higher than the highest Truth/Reality/Principle**

In the form of the world also,
In the form of Guru and disciple also,
In the form of Brahma (the Creator) also,
This Reality (Truth), higher than the highest,
manifests itself.

81

सत्यं जगदिति भानं संसृतये स्यादपक्वचित्तानाम् ।
तस्मादसत्यमेतन्निखिलं प्रतिपादयन्ति निगमान्ताः ॥ ८१ ॥

satyaṁ jagad-iti bhānaṁ saṁsṛtaye syād-apakva-
cittānām
tasmād-asatyam-etan-nikhilaṁ pratipādayanti
nigamāntāḥ

satyam jagat **the universe is real** iti bhanam **thus understanding** samsrtaye **for the cycle of birth and death/samsara** syat **will be** apakva-cittanam **for those of unripe minds** tasmat **hence** asatyam **unreal** etat-nikhilam **all this** pratipadayanti **declare** nigama-antah **the end of the Veda-s/Vedanta-s**

"The universe is real"—such understanding
By those of unripe minds will make for (lead to) samsara.
Hence, all the Vedanta-s declare,
"All this (universe) is unreal."

82

परिपक्वमानसानां पुरुषवराणां पुरातनैः सुकृतैः ।
ब्रह्मैवेदं सर्वं जगदिति भूयः प्रबोधयत्येषः ॥ ८२ ॥

paripakva-mānasānāṁ puruṣa-varāṇāṁ purātanaiḥ
sukṛtaiḥ
brahmaivedaṁ sarvaṁ jagad-iti bhūyaḥ
prabodhayaty-eṣaḥ

paripakva-manasanam **to those whose minds are well-ripened** purusa-varanam **the exalted ones** puratanaih-sukrtaih **by good deeds of the past** brahma-eva-idam **this is Brahman alone** sarvam jagat **the entire universe** iti **thus** bhuyah **again** prabodhayati **awakens** esah **this**

Those, whose minds are well ripened
By good deeds of the past, the exalted ones,
This (Vedanta) awakens again, thus:
"This, the entire universe, is Brahman alone."

83

अनवगतकाञ्चनानां भूषणधीरेव भूषणे हैमे ।
एवमविवेकभाजां जगति जनानां न तात्त्विकी धिषणा ॥ ८३ ॥

anavagata-kāñcanānāṁ bhūṣaṇa-dhīr-eva bhūṣaṇe haime
evam-aviveka-bhājāṁ jagati janānāṁ na tāttvikī dhiṣaṇā

anavagata-kancananam **for those not realizing the gold** bhusana-dhih-eva **only the perception of an ornament** bhusane haime **in a golden ornament** evam **in this way** aviveka-bhajam **for those that follow ignorance/no discrimination** jagati **in this world** jananam **for people** na tattviki dhisana **there is no understanding of the Reality (Truth)**

There is only the perception of an ornament
For those not realizing the gold in a golden ornament.
In this way, for the people of the world who follow ignorance (non-discrimination),
There is no understanding of the Reality (Truth).

84

अहमालम्बनसिद्धं कस्य परोक्षं भवेदिदं ब्रह्म ।
तदपि विचारविहीनैरपरोक्षयितुं न शक्यते मुग्धैः ॥ ८४ ॥

aham-ālambana-siddhaṁ kasya parokṣaṁ bhaved-
idaṁ brahma
tad-api vicāra-vihīnair-aparokṣayituṁ na śakyate
mugdhaiḥ

aham-alambana-siddham **that which can be attained by hanging onto "I"** kasya **for whom** paroksam **beyond perception/awareness** bhaved **(can) be** idam brahma **this Brahman** tad-api **even so** vicara-vihinaih **by those bereft of inquiry** aparoksayitum **to be directly aware of** na sakyate **is not possible** mugdhaih **by the ignorant**

For whom can this Brahman,
Attainable by hanging on to "I," be beyond
awareness?
Even so, to be directly aware of it is not possible
By the ignorant, bereft of inquiry.

85

अहमिदमिति च मतिभ्यां सततं व्यवहरति सर्वलोकोऽपि ।
प्रथमा प्रतीचि चरमा निवसति वपुरिन्द्रियादिबाह्यार्थे ॥ ८५ ॥

aham-idam-iti ca matibhyāṁ satataṁ vyavaharati
sarvaloko'pi
prathamā pratīci caramā nivasati vapur-indriyādi-
bāhyārthe

aham **"I"** idam **"this"** iti ca **and thus** matibhyam **by the ideas** satatam **always** vyavaharati **interacts** sarvalokah-api **all the world also** prathama **the first** pratici **is for the inward** carama **the last** nivasati **exists** vapuh-indriya-adi **in the body, senses and others** bahya-arthe **for the external**

"I," "this"—by such ideas
All the world also always interacts.
The first is for the inward,
And the last for the external such as the body,
the senses, and such.

86

वपुरिन्द्रियादिविषये याहंबुद्धिर्महत्यसौ भ्रान्तिः ।
तद्बुद्धिरतस्मिन्नित्यध्यासत्वेन शास्यमानत्वात् ॥ ८६ ॥

vapur-indriyādi-viṣaye yāhaṁ-buddhir-mahaty-asau
bhrāntiḥ
tad-buddhir-atasminn-ity-adhyāsatvena śāsyamānatvāt

vapuh-indriyadi-visaye **in respect of the body, senses** ya **that which** aham-buddhih **the conception of "I"** mahati-asau bhrantih **this is a huge misconception** tat-buddhih **that perception/conception** atasmin **not in that** iti **thus** adhyasatvena **by false attribution** sasyamanatvat **can be criticized**

In regard to the body and senses,
The conception of "I" is a huge misconception,
Because that conception can be criticized
That it falsely attributes what is not in that.

87

तस्मादशेषसाक्षी परमात्मैवाहमर्थ इत्युचितम् ।
अजडवदेव जडोऽयं सत्संबन्धाद्भवत्यहंकारः ॥ ८७ ॥

tasmād-aśeṣa-sākṣī paramātmaiv-āham-artha ity-
ucitam
a-jaḍavad-eva jaḍo'yaṁ sat-saṁbandhād-bhavaty-
ahaṁkāraḥ

tasmad **hence** asesa-saksi **the witness of all** paramatma-eva **is only the Supreme Self** aham-arthah **the meaning of "I"** iti **thus** ucitam **correct** a-jadavat-eva **like one who is not insentient** jadah-ayam **this insentient** sat-sambandhat **by connection with Reality** bhavati **becomes** ahamkarah **"I"-ness/ego**

The witness of all is only the Supreme Self—
This is the meaning of "I"—this is correct.
This insentient ("I"), by connection with Reality,
Becomes as if the sentient "I"-ness (ego).

88

तस्मात्सर्वशरीरेष्वहमहमित्येव भासते स्पष्टः ।
यः प्रत्ययो विशुद्धस्तस्य ब्रह्मैव भवति मुख्योऽर्थः ॥ ८८ ॥

tasmāt-sarva-śarīreṣv-aham-aham-ity-eva bhāsate spaṣṭaḥ
yaḥ pratyayo viśuddhas-tasya brahmaiva bhavati mukhyo'rthaḥ

tasmat **hence** sarva-sariresu **in all bodies** aham-aham **"I," "I"** iti **thus** eva **indeed** bhasate **shines** spastah **clearly** yah **which** pratyayah **conviction/conception** visuddhah **is clear** tasya **of that** brahma-eva **Brahman only** bhavati **becomes/is** mukhya-arthah **the direct meaning**

Hence, the conviction is clear:
What shines clearly in all bodies
Thus, as "I," "I"—
The direct meaning of that is Brahman alone.

89

गोशब्दार्थो गोत्वं तदपि व्यक्तिः प्रतीयतेऽर्थतया ।

अहमर्थः परमात्मा तद्वद्भ्रान्त्या भवत्यहंकारः ॥ ८९ ॥

go-śabd-ārtho gotvaṁ tad-api vyaktiḥ
pratīyate'rthatayā
aham-arthaḥ paramātmā tad-vad-bhrāntyā bhavaty-
ahaṁkāraḥ

go-sabda-arthah **the meaning of the word "cow"** gotvam **is cow-ness** tad-api **even then** vyaktih **the object** pratiyate **is indicated** artha-taya **by way of meaning** aham-arthah **the meaning of "I"** param-atma **the Supreme Self** tadvat **like that** bhrantya **by a misconception** bhavati **becomes** ahamkarah **'I'-ness/ the ego**

The meaning of the word "cow" relates to cowness,
Yet only the object (the cow) is indicated by way of
meaning.
The meaning of "I," the Supreme Self, likewise
Becomes, by misconception, the ego.

90

दग्धृत्वादिकमयसः पावकसङ्गेन भासते यद्वत् ।
तद्वच्चेतनसङ्गादहमि प्रतिभान्ति कर्तृतादीनि ॥ १० ॥

dagdhṛtvādikam-ayasaḥ pāvaka-saṅgena bhāsate yad-vat
tadvac-cetana-saṅgād-ahami pratibhānti kartṛt-ādīni

dagdhrtva-adikam **the capacity to burn and such** ayasah **of the iron** pavaka-sangena **by connection with the fire** bhasate **the manifest** yad-vat **just as** tad-vat **like that** cetana-sangat **by connection with Consciousness** ahami **in "I"** pratibhanti **manifest** kartrtva-adini **doership and such**

Just as the capacity to burn and such is manifest in the iron
By connection with fire,
Likewise, by connection with Consciousness,
Doership and such manifest themselves in "I."

91

देहेन्द्रियादिदृश्यव्यतिरिक्तं विमलमतुलमद्वैतम् ।
अहमर्थ इति विदित्वा तद्व्यतिरिक्तं न कल्पयेत्किंचित् ॥ ९१ ॥

dehendriyādi-dṛśya-vyatiriktaṁ vimalam-atulam-
advaitam
aham-artha iti viditvā tad-vyatiriktaṁ na kalpayet-
kiñcit

deha-indriya-adi **body, senses and others** drsya **objects** vyatiriktam **different** vimalam **pure/blemishless** atulam **incomparable** advaitam **without duality** aham-arthah **the meaning of "I"** iti **thus** viditva **knowing** tad-vyatiriktam **different therefrom** na kalpayet **one should not think of/suppose** kimcit **anything**

Different from the body, senses and other objects,
Pure (blemishless), incomparable, without duality—
Knowing the meaning of "I" to be thus,
One should not think of it as anything different
therefrom.

92

यद्वत्सुखदुःखानामवयवभेदादनेकता देहे ।
तद्वदिहासति भेदेऽप्यनुभववैविध्यमात्मनामेषाम् ॥ ९२ ॥

yad-vat-sukha-duḥkhānām-avayava-bhedād-anekatā dehe
tad-vad-ihāsati bhedepy-anubhava-vaividhyam-ātmanām-eṣām

yad-vat **just as** sukha-duhkhanam **of happiness and sorrow** avayava-bhedat **because of differences of limbs** anekata **variety** dehe **in the body** tad-vat **likewise** iha **here** asati **not existing** bhede-api **in difference also** (another version reads: sati-abheda **existing in non-difference)** anubhava **experience** vaividhyam **variety** atmanam **of the selves** esam **of these**

Just as there is variety of happiness and sorrow
In the body, because of differences of limbs,
Likewise, here, also not existing in difference
(or existing in nondifference)
Is the experience by (of) the variety of these
[individual] "selves."

93

किमिदं किमस्य रूपं कथमिदमासीदमुष्य को हेतुः ।
इति न कदापि विचिन्त्यं चिन्त्यं मायेति धीमता विश्वम् ॥ ९३ ॥

kim-idaṁ kim-asya rūpaṁ katham-idam-āsīd-amuṣya
ko hetuḥ
iti na kadāpi vicintyaṁ cintyaṁ māyeti dhīmatā
viśvam

kim-idam **"what is this"** kim-asya rupam **"what is its nature"** katham-idam asit **"how was this"** amusya ko hetuh **"what is its origin"** iti **thus** na kadapi **never** vicintyam **should be thought of** cintyam **it should be thought of** maya-iti **that it is delusion** dhimata **by the wise** visvam **this universe**

"What is this?" "What is its nature?" "How was
this?" "What is its origin?"
It should never be thought of thus.
It should be considered by the wise
That this universe is a delusion.

94

दन्तिनि दारुविकारे दारु तिरोभवति सोऽपि तत्रैव ।
जगति तथा परमात्मा परमात्मन्यपि जगत्तिरोधत्ते ॥ ९४ ॥

dantini dāru-vikāre dāru tirobhavati so'pi tatraiva
jagati tathā paramātmā paramātmany-api jagat-
tirodhatte

dantini daru-vikare **in the wood shaped as an elephant** daru **the wood** tiro-bhavati **disappears** sah-api **that also (the elephant)** tatra-eva **is like that too** jagati **in the universe** tatha **likewise** paramatma **the Supreme Self** paramatmani-api **and in the Supreme Self also** jagat **the universe** tirodhatte **disappears**

In the wood shaped as an elephant,
Wood disappears, so also that (elephant), too;
Likewise, in the universe, the Supreme Self,
And, in the Supreme Self, also, the universe,
disappear.

95

आत्ममये महति पटे विविधजगच्चित्रमात्मना लिखितम् ।
स्वयमेव केवलमसौ पश्यन्प्रमुदं प्रयाति परमात्मा ॥ ९५ ॥

ātma-maye mahati paṭe vividha-jagac-citram-ātmanā likhitam
svayam-eva kevalam-asau paśyan-pramudaṁ prayāti paramātmā

atma-maye **full of the Self** mahati **vast** pate **on the cloth** vividha-jagat **of the variegated universe** citram **picture** atmana **by the Self** likhitam **is painted** svayam-eva **by itself** kevalam **that which alone is** asau **this** pasyan **seeing** pramudam **delight** prayati **reaches** paramatma **the Supreme Self**

The picture of the variegated universe
Is painted by the Self itself on the vast cloth that is the Self.
The Supreme Self, that which alone is,
Reaches delight seeing this.

96

चिन्मात्रममलमक्षयमद्वयमानन्दमनुभवारूढम् ।
ब्रह्मैवास्ति तदन्यन्न किमप्यस्तीति निश्चयो विदुषाम् ॥ ९६ ॥

cin-mātram-amalam-akṣayam-advayam-ānandam-anubhav-ārūḍham
brahmaiv-āsti tad-anyan-na kimapy-astīti niścayo viduṣām

cid-matram **just Consciousness** amalam **without blemish** aksayam **undecaying** advayam **without a second** anandam **Bliss** anubhava-arudham **to be attained by direct experience** brahma-eva **only Brahman** asti **exists** tat-anyat **apart from That** na kim-api **nothing else** asti **exists** iti **thus** niscayah **certitude** vidusam **of the realized ones**

Just Consciousness, blemishless, undecaying,
Without a second, Bliss, to be attained by direct experience—
Brahman alone exists. Apart from That, nothing else exists.
This is the certitude of the realized ones.

97

व्यवहारस्य दशेयं विद्याविद्येति भेदपरिभाषा ।

नास्त्येव तत्त्वदृष्ट्या तत्त्वं ब्रह्मैव नान्यदस्त्यस्मात् ॥ १७ ॥

vyavahārasya daśeyaṁ vidyā-vidyeti bheda-paribhāṣā
nāsty-eva tattva-dṛṣṭyā tattvaṁ brahmaiva nānyad-
asty-asmāt

vyavaharasya dasa-iyam **this is the customary stage/state of common, everyday life/the stage of argumentation** vidya-avidya-iti bhedah-paribhasa **differences of technical phraseology such as knowledge and non-knowledge (ignorance)** nasti-eva **it does not exist** tattva-drstya **from the point of view of Truth** tattvam **the Truth** brahma-eva **is only Brahman** na-anyat **nothing else** asti-asmat **exists (different) from this**

Differences in terminology, such as knowledge and ignorance,
Exist in this state of common, everyday life.*
They do not exist from the standpoint of Truth.
Brahman is the only Truth, and nothing else exists different therefrom.

*Alt. trans.: Exist at this stage of argumentation.

98

अस्त्यन्यदिति मतं चेत्तदपि ब्रह्मैतदस्तितारूपम् ।
व्यतिरिक्तमस्तिताया नास्तितया शून्यमेव तत्सिद्धम् ॥ ९८ ॥

asty-anyad-iti mataṁ cet-tad-api brahmaitad-astitā-
rūpam
vyatiriktam-astitāyā nāstitayā śūnyam-eva tat-siddham

asti-anyat **something else exists** iti **thus** matam cet **if there is an idea** tad-api **that also** brahma **is Brahman** etat-astita-rupam **this is the nature of Existence** vyatiriktam astitaya **different from Existence** nastitaya **by nonexistence** sunyam-eva **only a void** tat **that** siddham **is certain**

If there is an idea that something else exists,
That also is Brahman, because it is of the nature of
Existence.
If it is different from Existence,
It is certain that it is only a void, because of non-
existence.

99

तत्त्वावबोधशक्त्या सुस्थितया बाधितापि सा माया ।
आदेहपातमेषामाभात्यात्मानमपि निजं विदुषाम् ॥ ९९ ॥

tattv-āvabodha-śaktyā su-sthitayā bādhitāpi sā māyā
ā-deha-pātam-eṣām-ābhāty-ātmānam-api nijaṁ
vidusām

tattva **Truth** avabodha-saktya **by the power of Knowledge** su-sthitaya **being well established** badhitah-api **even though overcome** sa maya **that delusion** a-deha-patam **until the fall of the body** esam **of them** abhati **shines** atmanam-api **their Self also** nijam **own** vidusam **for the realized ones**

Even delusion having been overcome
By the well established power of the Knowledge
of Truth,
For the realized ones, until the fall of the body,
Their own Self also continues to shine.

100

एष विशेषो विदुषां पश्यन्तोऽपि प्रपञ्चसंसारम् ।
पृथगात्मनो न किंचित्पश्येयुः सकलनिगमनिर्णीतात् ॥ १०० ॥

eṣa viśeṣo viduṣāṁ paśyanto'pi prapañca-saṁsāram
pṛthag-ātmano na kiṁcit-paśyeyuḥ sakala-nigama-
nirṇītāt

esa visesah **this is the speciality** vidusam **of the realized ones** pasyantah-api **even though looking at** prapanca-samsaram **this phenomenal samsara** prthak **as separate/different from** atmanah **the Self** na kimcit **nothing at all** pasyeyuh **they will see** sakala **all** nigama **Veda-s** nirnitat **by understanding**

This is the speciality of the realized:
Though looking at the phenomenal samsara,
They will see nothing at all
As different from the Self, as understood from all the Veda-s.

101

किं चिन्त्यं किमचिन्त्यं किं कथनीयं किमप्यकथनीयम् ।
किं कृत्यं किमकृत्यं निखिलं ब्रह्मेति जानतां विदुषाम् ॥ १०१ ॥

kiṁ cintyaṁ kim-acintyaṁ kiṁ kathanīyaṁ kimapy-akathanīyam
kiṁ kṛtyaṁ kim-akṛtyaṁ nikhilaṁ brahmeti jānatāṁ viduṣām

kim cintyam **what is there to think of** kim-acintyam **what is there not to be thought of** kim kathaniyam **what is there to speak of** kim-api-akathaniyam **and what is there not to speak of** kim krtyam **what is to be done** kim-akrtyam **what is not to be done** nikhilam **all** brahma **is Brahman** iti **thus** janatam **knowing** vidusam **for the realized ones**

What is there to think, what is there not to think,
What is there to speak, what is there not to speak,
What is there to be done, what is there not to be done,
For the realized ones who know that all is Brahman?

102

निखिलं दृश्यविशेषं दृग्रूपत्वेन पश्यतां विदुषाम् ।
बन्धो नापि न मुक्तिर्न परात्मत्वं न चापि जीवत्वम् ॥ १०२ ॥

nikhilaṁ dṛśya-viśeṣaṁ dṛg-rūpatvena paśyatāṁ
viduṣām
bandho nāpi na muktir-na parātmatvaṁ na cāpi
jīvatvam

nikhilam **all** drsya-visesam **objects of diverse attributes** drg-rupatvena **to be of the nature of the seer (the Self)** pasyatam **who see** vidusam **for the realized ones** bandhah na **no bondage** api na muktih **and also no liberation** na paratmatvam **no Supreme Self-hood** na ca-api jivatvam **and also no jiva (individual self)-hood**

For the realized ones who see
All objects of diverse attributes to be of the nature of the seer (the Self),
There is no bondage and also no liberation,
No state of the Supreme Self and also no state of individuality (state of being a jiva).

103

असकृदनुचिन्तितानामव्याहततरनिजोपदेशानाम् ।
प्रामाण्यपरमसीम्नां निगमनमिदमेव निखिलनिगमानाम् ॥ १०३ ॥

asakṛd-anucintitānām-avyāhata-tara-nijopadeśānām
prāmāṇya-parama-sīmnāṁ nigamanam-idam-eva
nikhila-nigamānām

asakrt **all the time, continuously** anucintitanam **for those who think after/inquire** avyahata-tara **without the least contradiction** nija-upadesanam **conveying their own teaching** pramanya **of authority** parama-simnam **the ultimate frontier** nigamanam **conclusion** idam-eva **this only** nikhila **all** nigamanam **of the Veda-s**

For those who inquire continuously,
Only this is the conclusion of all the Veda-s,
The ultimate frontier of authority,
Conveying their own teaching without the least contradiction.

104

इति बोधितः स गुरुणा शिष्यो हृष्टः प्रणम्य तं पदयोः ।
स्वानुभवसिद्धमर्थं स्वयमेवान्तर्विचारयामास ॥ १०४ ॥

iti bodhitaḥ sa guruṇā śiṣyo hṛṣṭaḥ praṇamya taṁ padayoḥ
svānubhava-siddham-arthaṁ svayamev-āntar-vicārayāmāsa

iti bodhitah **thus taught** sah **he** guruna **by the Guru** sisyah **the disciple** hrstah **full of joy** pranamya **prostrating** tam **him** padayoh **at the feet** sva-anubhava-siddham **established by his own experience** artham **significance** svayam-eva **by himself** antah **within himself** vicarayamasa **meditated upon/inquired into**

Thus taught by the Guru,
The disciple, full of joy, and prostrating at his feet,
Meditated upon (inquired into), by and within himself,
The significance established by his own experience.

105

अजरोऽहमक्षरोऽहं प्राज्ञोऽहं प्रत्यगात्मबोधोऽहम् ।
परमानन्दमयोऽहं परमशिवोऽहं भवामि परिपूर्णः ॥ १०५ ॥

ajaro'ham-akṣaro'haṁ prājño'haṁ pratyag-ātma-
bodho'ham
paramānanda-mayo'haṁ parama-śivo'haṁ bhavāmi
paripūrṇaḥ

ajarah-aham **I am un-aging** aksarah-aham **I am undecaying** prajnah-aham **I have exalted Knowledge** pratyagatma-bodhah-aham **I am the Knowledge that is the inner Self** parama-ananda-mayah-aham **I am full of the supreme Bliss** parama-sivah aham **I am the Supreme Siva** bhavami paripurnah **I am the perfectly Full and Complete**

I am un-aging. I am undecaying. I have exalted
Knowledge.
I am the Knowledge that is the inner Self.
I am full of Supreme Bliss. I am the Supreme Siva.
I am the perfectly Full and Complete.

106

आद्योऽहमात्मभाजामात्मानन्दानुभूतिरसिकोऽहम् ।

आबालगोपमखिलैरहमित्यनुभूयमानमहिमाहम् ॥ १०६ ॥

ādyo'ham-ātma-bhājām-ātmānand-ānubhūti-
rasiko'ham
ābāla-gopam-akhilair-aham-ity-anubhūyamāna-
mahimāham

adyah-aham **I am the foremost** atma-bhajam **of those who resort to the Self** atma-ananda-anubhuti **the Awareness/direct Knowledge of the Bliss of the Self** rasikah-aham **I am the enjoyer** abala-gopam-akhilaih **by all down to/including children and the illiterate/cowherd** aham **"I"** iti **thus** anubhuyamana **enjoyable** mahima **glory** aham **I am**

I am the foremost among those resorting to the Self.
I am the enjoyer of the Awareness of the Bliss of
the Self.
I am the glory that is enjoyed as "I"
By all, including the children and the illiterate.

107

इहपरसुखविमुखोऽहं निजसुखबोधानुभूतिभरितोऽहम् ।
इतिमतिदूरतरोऽहं भावेतरसुखनिषक्तचित्तोऽहम् ॥ १०७ ॥

iha-para-sukha-vimukho'haṁ nija-sukha-bodh-
ānubhūti-bharito'ham
iti-mati-dūra-taro'haṁ bhāvetara-sukha-niṣakta-
citto'ham

iha-para-sukha **the joys of here and beyond** vimukhah-aham **I turn my face away from** nija sukha **my own joy** bodha **Knowledge** anubhuti **awareness** bharitah-aham **I am filled with** iti-mati **the idea that this is so** duratarah-aham **I am very far removed from** bhava-itara **a conviction that is otherwise** sukha **happy** nisakta-cittah-aham **I am of the mind fixed in/united with**

I turn my face away from the joys of the "here" and "beyond."
I am filled with my own joy of the Awareness of Knowledge.
I am very far removed from the idea that a thing is thus.
I am of the happy mind that is united with a different conviction.*

*Alt. trans.: I am of the mind with a conviction that joy is otherwise.

108

ईशोऽहमीश्वराणामीर्ष्याद्वेषानुषङ्गरहितोऽहम् ।
ईक्षणविषयमतीनामीप्सितपुरुषार्थसाधनपरोऽहम् ॥ १०८ ॥

īśo'ham-īśvarāṇām-īrṣyā-dveṣ-ānuṣaṅga-rahito'ham
īkṣaṇa-viṣaya-matīnām-īpsita-puruṣārtha-sādhana-paro'ham

isah-aham-isvaranam **I am the Lord of the Lords** irsya **jealousy** dvesa **hatred** anusanga **connection/ association with** rahitah-aham **I am devoid of** iksana-visaya **in the matter of seeing** matinam **for those who have their minds on** ipsita **desired** purusartha **aim of human life** sadhanaparah-aham **I have the goal of/am intent on fulfilling**

I am the Lord of the Lords.
I am devoid of connection to jealousy and hatred.
For those who have their minds set on seeing [the Truth],
I am intent on the fulfillment of the desired aim of human life.

109

उदयोऽहमेव जगतामुपनिषदुद्यानकृतविहारोऽहम् ।
उद्वेलशोकसागरबाडबमुखहव्यवाहनार्चिरहम् ॥ १०९ ॥

udayo'ham-eva jagatām-upaniṣad-udyāna-kṛta-
vihāro'ham
udvela-śoka-sāgara-bāḍaba-mukha-havyavāhan-ārcir-
aham

udayah-aham **I am the origin** jagatam **of the universe** upanisad-udyana **in the garden of the Upanisad-s** krta-viharah-aham **I am he who sports** udvela **overflowing** soka-sagara **ocean of sorrow** badaba-mukha **submarine fire** havyavahana-arcih aham **I am the tongue of flame**

I am the origin of the universe.
I am he who sports in the garden of the Upanisad-s.
I am the tongue of flame of the submarine fire
For the overflowing ocean of sorrow.

110

ऊर्जस्वलनिजविभवैरूर्ध्वमधस्तिर्यगश्नुवानोऽहम् ।
ऊहापोहविचारैरूररीकृतवत्प्रतीयमानोऽहम् ॥ ११० ॥

ūrjasvala-nija-vibhavair-ūrdhvam-adhas-tiryag-
aśnuvāno'ham
ūhāpoha-vicārair-urarī-kṛta-vat-pratīyamāno'ham

urjasvala **mighty** nija-vibhavaih **by own glories** urdhvam **above** adhah **below** tiryak **across** asnuvanah-aham **I am he who pervades** uhapoha-vicaraih **by an inquiry into the pros and cons/by examination, removing, and inquiry/by comprehending, reasoning, and inquiry** urari-krta-vat **as if accepted** pratiyamanah-aham **I am he who is proved**

I am He who pervades above, below, and across,
By my own mighty glory.
I am He who is proved, as if accepted,
By means of an inquiry into the pros and cons.*

*Alt. trans.: By examination, removing, and inquiry./
By comprehending, reasoning, and inquiry.

111

ऋषिरहमृष्यगणोऽहं दृष्टिरहं दृश्यमानमहमेव ।
ऋद्धिरहं वृद्धिरहं तृप्तिरहं तृप्तिदीपदीप्तिरहम् ॥ १११ ॥

ṛṣir-aham-ṛṣya-gaṇo'haṁ dṛṣṭir-ahaṁ dṛśyamānam-aham-eva
ṛddhir-ahaṁ vṛddhir-ahaṁ tṛptir-ahaṁ tṛpti-dīpa-dīptir-aham

rsih-aham **I am the seer** rsyaganah-aham **I am the host of seers** drstih-aham **I am the seeing** drsyamanam-aham-eva **I am the one to be seen also** rddhih-aham **I am accomplished** vrddhih-aham **I am growth** trptih-aham **I am satisfaction** trpti-dipah-diptih-aham **I am the glow of the light of satisfaction**

I am the seer. I am the host of seers.
I am the seeing. I am the one to be seen, also.
I am the accomplishment. I am the growth.
I am the satisfaction. I am the glow of the light of satisfaction.

112

एकोऽहमेतदीदृशमेवमितिस्फुरितभेदरहितोऽहम् ।
एष्टव्योऽहमनीहैरन्तः सुकृतानुभूतिभूतोऽहम् ॥ ११२ ॥

eko'ham-etad-īdṛśam-evam-iti-sphurita-bheda-
rahito'ham
eṣṭavyo'ham-anīhair-antaḥ sukṛt-ānubhūti-bhūto'ham

ekah-aham **I am the One** etad **"this'"** idrsam **"like this"** evam **"in this way"** iti **thus** sphurita **vibrating/unsteady** bheda **differences** rahitah-aham **I am devoid of** estavyah-aham **I am the one to be approached** anihaih **by the desireless** antah **internal/inside** sukrta **by meritorious acts** anubhuti-bhutah-aham **I am the being who has Awareness/direct Knowledge**

I am the One; I am devoid of the unsteady differences
Such as "this," "like this," "in this way," or thus.
I am the one within, who is to be approached by the desireless,
Having done meritorious deeds; I am the being who has Awareness.

113

ऐक्यावभासकोऽहं वाक्यपरिज्ञानपावनमतीनाम् ।
ऐशमहमेव तत्त्वं नैशतमःप्रायमोहमिहिरोऽहम् ॥ ११३ ॥

aiky-āvabhāsako'haṁ vākya-parijñāna-pāvana-
matīnām
aiśam-aham-eva tattvaṁ naiśa-tamaḥ-prāya-moha-
mihiro'ham

aikya **Oneness** avabhasakah-aham **I am the one who reveals/illumines/makes manifest** vakya-parijnana **the thorough knowledge of the aphorisms** pavana **purified** matinam **minds** aisam **of the Lord** aham-eva **I alone am** tattvam **the Reality** na-isa **non-existence of the Lord** tamah **of the darkness** prayah **like** moha-mihirah-aham **I am the sun for the delusion**

I am the one who reveals Oneness
To those minds purified by the thorough knowledge of the aphorisms.
I alone am the Reality of the Lord.
I am like the sun for the darkness of the delusion of the nonexistence of the Lord.

114

ओजोऽहमोषधीनामोतप्रोतायमानभुवनोऽहम् ।
ओंकारसारसोल्लसदात्मसुखामोदमत्तभृङ्गोऽहम् ॥ ११४ ॥

ojo'ham-oṣadhīnām-otaprotāyamāna-bhuvano'ham
oṁkāra-sāras-ollasad-ātma-sukhā-moda-matta-
bhṛṅgo'ham

ojah **the potency** aham **I am** osadhinam **of the herbs** ota-protayamana **woven lengthwise and crosswise** bhuvanah-aham **I am the world** omkara **the syllable Om** sarasa **of the lake** ullasat **delighted** atma-sukha **happiness of the Self** amoda **joy** matta **intoxicated** bhrngah-aham **I am the bee**

I am the potency of the herbs.
I am the warp and woof of the world.
I am the intoxicated bee delighted with the joy
Of the happiness of the Self in the lake of Om
(Pranava).

115

औषधमहमशुभानामौपाधिकधर्मजालरहितोऽहम् ।
औदार्यातिशयोऽहं विविधचतुर्वर्गवितरणपरोऽहम् ॥ ११५ ॥

auṣadham-aham-aśubhānām-aupādhika-dharma-jāla-
rahito'ham
audāry-ātiśayo'haṁ vividha-caturvarga-vitaraṇa-
paro'ham

ausadham-aham **I am the balm** asubhanam **for evils** aupadhika **the conditioning** dharma-jala **web of qualities** rahitah aham **I am devoid of** audarya **of generosity** atisayah-aham **I am the abundance** vividha **the various** caturvarga **four goals of human life** vitarana-parah-aham **I am intent on granting**

I am the balm for evils.
I am devoid of the conditioning web of qualities.
I am the abundance of generosity.
I am intent on granting, in variety, the four goals of human life.[1]

---

[1] *Dharma (righteousness), kama (desire), artha (prosperity), and Moksa (Liberation).*

116

अङ्कुशमहमखिलानां महत्तया मत्तवारणेन्द्राणाम् ।
अम्बरमिव विमलोऽहं शम्बररिपुजातविकृतिरहितोऽहम् ॥ ११६ ॥

aṅkuśam-aham-akhilānāṁ mahattayā matta-
    vāraṇendrāṇām
ambaram-iva vimalo'haṁ śambara-ripu-jāta-vikṛti-
    rahito'ham

ankusam-aham **I am the goad** akhilanam **of all** mahat-taya **by (my) greatness** matta-varana-indranam **of all mighty elephants in rut** ambaram iva **like the space** vimalah-aham **I am blemishless** sambara-ripu **the god of love** jata **generated by** vikrti-rahitah-aham **I am devoid of changes**

I am, by my greatness, the goad
Of all mighty elephants in rut.
I am blemishless like space.
I am devoid of the changes generated by the god
    of love.

117

अस्तविकल्पमतीनामस्खलदुपदेशगम्यमानोऽहम् ।
अस्थिरसुखविमुखोऽहं सुस्थिरसुखबोधसंपदुचितोऽहम् ॥ ११७॥

asta-vikalpa-matīnām-askhalad-upadeśa-
gamyamāno'ham
asthira-sukha-vimukho'haṁ su-sthira-sukha-bodha-
saṁpad-ucito'ham

asta **decadent** vikalpa **erroneous/doubts** matinam **for those of ideas** askhalat **firm, undeviating** upadesa **by instruction** gamyamanah-aham **I am one who is reached** asthira **unsteady/fickle** sukha **joy** vimukhah aham **I am he who turns his face away** su-sthira **ever firm** sukha **joy** bodha **Knowledge** sampat **plenty** ucitah-aham **I am the fit one**

I am one who is reached by undeviating instruction
For those of decadent, erroneous ideas.
I am one who turns his face away from fickle joy.
I am the fit one for the plentitude of ever firm joy
and Knowledge.

118

करुणारसभरितोऽहं कबलितकमलासनादिलोकोऽहम् ।
कलुषाकृतिविधुरोऽहं कल्मषसुकृतोपलेपरहितोऽहम् ॥ ११८ ॥

karuṇā-rasa-bharito'haṁ kabalita-kamalāsanādi-
loko'ham
kaluṣ-ākṛti-vidhuro'haṁ kalmaṣa-sukṛt-opalepa-
rahito'ham

karuna-rasa **the essence of compassion** bharitah-aham **I am filled with** kabalita **devoured** kamalasana-adi **the lotus-seated and such (of Brahma)** lokah **worlds** aham **I am** kalusa **blemish** akrtih **having a form** vidhurah-aham **I am far from** kalmasa-sukrta **the wicked and the virtuous** upalepa **covering** rahitah-aham **I am free from**

I am filled with the essence of compassion.
I am one who has devoured the worlds of the lotus-seated (Brahma) and others.
I am far from having a form with blemish.
I am free from any covering of wickedness or virtue.

119

खानामगोचरोऽहं खातीतोऽहं खपुष्पभवगोऽहम् ।

खलजनदुरासदोऽहं खण्डज्ञानापनोदनपरोऽहम् ॥ ११९ ॥

khānām-agocaro'haṁ khātīto'haṁ kha-puṣpa-
bhavago'ham
khala-jana-durāsado'haṁ khaṇḍa-jñān-āpanodana-
paro'ham

khanam **of the organs of sense** agocarah-aham **I am beyond the range** kha-atitah-aham **I transcend the sky** kha-puspa **flower in the sky (nonexistent)** bhavagah-aham **I am the pervader** khala-jana **wicked people** dur-asadah-aham **I am difficult to approach** khanda-jnana **the knowledge of the fragmented** apanodana-parah-aham **I am intent on dispelling**

I am beyond the range of the organs of sense.
I transcend the sky, and I am the pervader of the
flower in the sky (the nonexistent phenomenal
world).
For the wicked, I am difficult to approach.
I am intent on dispelling the knowledge of the
fragmented.

120

गलितद्वैतकथोऽहं देहीभवदखिलमूलहृदयोऽहम् ।
गन्तव्योऽहमनीहैर्गत्यागतिरहितपूर्णबोधोऽहम् ॥ १२० ॥

galita-dvaita-katho'haṁ dehī-bhavad-akhila-mūla-
hṛdayo'ham
gantavyo'ham-anīhair-gatyāgati-rahita-pūrṇa-
bodho'ham

galita **slipped away** dvaita **duality** kathah **talk** aham **I am** dehi-bhavat **being the Self (the occupier of the body)** akhila-mula-hrdayah-aham **I am the heart that is the source of all** gantavyah-aham **I am the one to be reached** anihaih **by the desireless** gati-agati **going and coming** rahita **devoid of** purna-bodhah-aham **I am the perfect Knowledge**

I am one from whom the talk of duality has slipped away.
Being the Self, I am the heart, which is the source of all.
I am the one to be reached by the desireless.
I am the perfect Knowledge devoid of going and coming.

121

घनतरविमोहतिमिरप्रकरप्रध्वंसभानुनिकरोऽहम् ।
घटिकावासररजनीवत्सरयुगकल्पकालभेदोऽहम् ॥ १२१ ॥

ghana-tara-vimoha-timira-prakara-pradhvaṁsa-
bhānu-nikaro'ham
ghaṭikā-vāsara-rajanī-vatsara-yuga-kalpa-kāla-
bhedo'ham

ghana-tara **very dense** vimoha **delusion** timira-prakara **concentration of darkness** pradhvamsa **destroying** bhanu-nikarah-aham **I am the multitude of suns** ghatika **a period of time (24 minutes)** vasara **a day** rajani **a night** vatsara **a year** yuga **millions of years** kalpa **the life period of Brahma (1000 yugas)** kala-bhedah-aham **I am the divisions of time**

I am the multitude of suns for the destruction
Of the concentration of darkness of very dense
delusion.
I am the divisions of time such as
Ghatika, day, night, year, yuga (an age), and kalpa.

122

चरदचरदात्मकोऽहं चतुरमतिश्लाघनीयचरितोऽहम् ।

चपलजनदुर्गमोऽहं चञ्चलभवजलधिपारदेशोऽहम् ॥ १२२ ॥

carad-acarad-ātmako'haṁ catura-mati-ślāghanīya-
carito'ham
capala-jana-durgamo'haṁ cañcala-bhava-jaladhi-pāra-
deśo'ham

carat-acarat **the moving and the unmoving** atmakah aham **I have within me** catura-mati **sharp-witted** slaghaniya **extolled** caritah-aham **I am one with deeds/a history of deeds** capala-jana **fickle persons** durgamah-aham **I am difficult of access/unattainable** cancala **moving/unsteady** bhava-jaladhi **ocean of mundane existence** para-desah-aham **I am the far shore**

I have within me the moving and the unmoving.
I am the one with deeds extolled by the sharp-witted.
For fickle people, I am difficult of access.
I am the far shore of the unsteady ocean of mundane existence.

123

छन्दःसिन्धुनिगूढज्ञानसुखास्वादमोदमानोऽहम् ।
छलपदविहितमतीनां छन्नोऽहं शान्तिमार्गगम्योऽहम् ॥ १२३ ॥

chandaḥ-sindhu-nigūḍha-jñāna-sukhāsvāda-
modamāno'ham
chala-pada-vihita-matīnāṁ channo'haṁ śānti-mārga-
gamyo'ham

chandah-sindhu **the ocean of the Veda-s** nigudha **hidden** jnana-sukha **the joy of Knowledge** asvada **relishing** modamanah-aham **I am one who is happy** chala-pada **deceptive words** vihita-matinam **minds possessed of** channah-aham **I am veiled from** santi marga **by the path of peace** gamyah-aham **I am to be reached**

I am one who is happy relishing the joy
Of Knowledge hidden in the ocean of the Veda-s.
I am veiled from minds possessed of deceptive
words.
I am to be reached by the path of peace.

124

जलजासनादिगोचरपञ्चमहाभूतमूलभूतोऽहम् ।
जगदानन्दकरोऽहं जन्मजरामरणरोगरहितोऽहम् ॥ १२४ ॥

jalajāsanādi-gocara-pañca-mahābhūta-mūla-bhūto'ham
jagad-ānanda-karo'haṁ janma-jarā-maraṇa-roga-
rahito'ham

jalajasana-adi **the lotus-seated Brahma and others** gocara **range** panca-maha-bhuta **the five great elements** mula-bhutah-aham **I am the one that is the root** jagad-ananda-karah-aham **I am the one who makes the universe blissful** janma **birth** jara **old age** marana **death** roga **disease** rahitah-aham **I am devoid of**

I am the one that is the root of the range of things,
From the lotus-seated (Brahma) and others to the
five great elements.[1]
I am the one who makes the universe blissful.
I am devoid of birth, old age, death, and disease.

---

[1] *Space, air, fire, water, earth.*

125

झंकृतिहुंकृतिशिञ्जितबृंहितमुखविविधनादभेदोऽहम् ।
झटितिघटितात्मवेदनदीपपरिस्फुरितहृदयभवनोऽहम् ॥ १२५ ॥

jhaṁkṛti-huṁkṛti-śiñjita-bṛṁhita-mukha-vividha-nāda-
bhedo'ham
jhaṭiti-ghaṭit-ātma-vedana-dīpa-parisphurita-hṛdaya-
bhavano'ham

jhamkrti **jingling** humkrti **bellowing** sinjita **tinkling** brmhita **roaring** mukha **mouth** vividha **various** nada-bhedah-aham **I am the different sounds** jhatiti **quickly** ghatita **made up** atma-vedana **Self-Realization** dipa **lamp** parisphurita **shining** hrdaya bhavanah **mansion of the heart** aham **I am**

I am the variety of different sounds such as
Jingling, tinkling, bellowing, and those of a roaring
mouth.
I am the one illuminating the mansion of the heart
By the lamp of Self-Realization quickly lit.

126

ज्ञानमहं ज्ञेयमहं ज्ञाताहं ज्ञानसाधनगणोऽहम् ।
ज्ञातृज्ञानज्ञेयविनाकृतमस्तित्वमात्रमेवाहम् ॥ १२६ ॥

jñānam-ahaṁ jñeyam-ahaṁ jñātāhaṁ jñāna-sādhana-gaṇo'ham
jñātṛ-jñāna-jñeya-vinā-kṛtam-astitva-mātram-evāham

jnanam-aham **I am knowledge** jneyam-aham **I am the one to be known** jnata-aham **I am the knower** jnana-sadhana-ganah-aham **I am the group of practices for the means of acquiring Knowledge** jnatr-jnana-jneya **the knower, the knowing, and (the thing) to be known** vina-krtam **made without (these)** astitva-matrah **just Existence** eva-aham **indeed I am**

I am the knowledge, the knower, and the one to be known.
I am the group of practices for the means of acquiring Knowledge.
I am, indeed, just Existence, without anything of
"Knower," "knowledge," or "[the thing] to be known."

127

तत्त्वातीतपदोऽहं तनुरहमस्मीति भावरहितोऽहम् ।
तामसदुरधिगमोऽहं तत्त्वंपदबोधबोध्यहृदयोऽहम् ॥ १२७ ॥

tattv-ātīta-pado'haṁ tanur-aham-asmīti bhāva-
rahito'ham
tāmasa-dur-adhigamo'haṁ tat-tvaṁ-pada-bodha-
bodhya-hṛdayo'ham

tattva-atita **transcending the tattva-s (factors of experience)** padah-aham **I am the state** tanuh **the body** aham-asmi **I am** iti **thus** bhava-rahitah-aham **I am devoid of the attitude** tamasa **[by] the ignorant** dur-adhigamah-aham **I am difficult of mastery** tat **That** tvam **you** pada **word** bodha **Knowledge** bodhya **aware of/knows of** hrdayah-aham **I am the heart**

I am the state transcending the tattva-s.
I am devoid of the attitude that I am the body.
I am difficult of mastery by the ignorant.
I am the Heart aware of the Knowledge of the words
"That" and "you."

128

दैवतदैत्यनिशाचरमानवतिर्यङ्महीधरादिरहम् ।
देहेन्द्रियरहितोऽहं दक्षिणपूर्वादिदिग्विभागोऽहम् ॥१२८ ॥

daivata-daitya-niśācara-mānava-tiryaṅ-mahī-dharādir-
aham
deh-endriya-rahito'haṁ dakṣiṇa-pūrvādi-dig-
vibhāgo'ham

daivata **of deities** daitya **demons** nisacara **fiends** manava **men** tiryak **animals** mahidhara **mountains** adih-aham **I am the foremost** deha-indriya **body and senses** rahitah-aham **I am devoid of** daksina **south** purva **east** adi **and others** dig-vibhagah-aham **I am the division of directions**

I am the foremost of all deities, demons,
Fiends, men, animals, and mountains.
I am devoid of body and senses.
I am the division of directions like south, east,
and others.

129

धर्माधर्ममयोऽहं धर्माधर्मादिबन्धरहितोऽहम् ।
धार्मिकजनसुलभोऽहं धन्योऽहं धातुरादिभूतोऽहम् ॥१२९ ॥

dharm-ādharma-mayo'haṁ dharm-ādharmādi-
bandha-rahito'ham
dhārmika-jana-sulabho'haṁ dhanyo'haṁ dhātur-
ādi-bhūto'ham

dharma-adharma-mayah-aham **I am of the nature of right and wrong** dharma-adharma-adi **(of) right and wrong and such** bandha-rahitah-aham **I am devoid of the bondage** dharmika-jana **(for) righteous men** sulabhah-aham **I am easily attainable** dhanyah-aham **I am the fortunate/happy** dhatuh **of the Creator** adi-bhutah-aham **I am the origin**

I am of the nature of right and wrong.
I am devoid of the bondage of right and wrong and such.
I am easily attainable by righteous men.
I am fortunate (happy). I am the origin of the Creator.

130

नामादिविरहितोऽहं नरकस्वर्गापवर्गरहितोऽहम् ।
नादान्तवेदितोऽहं नानाविधनिखिलनिगमसारोऽहम् ॥ १३० ॥

nāmādi-virahito'haṁ naraka-svarg-āpavarga-rahito'ham
nādānta-vedito'haṁ nānā-vidha-nikhila-nigama-sāro'ham

nama-adi **names and such** virahitah-aham **I am devoid of** naraka **hell** svarga **heaven** apavarga **final beatitude/final emancipation** rahitah-aham **I am devoid of** nada-anta **the end of primordial sound** veditah-aham **I am the one known as** nana-vidha **various** nikhila **all** nigama-sarah-aham **I am the essence of the Veda-s**

I am devoid of names and such.
I am devoid of hell or heaven or final beatitude (final emancipation).
I am the one known as the end of the primordial sound.
I am the essence of all the various Veda-s.

131

परजीवभेदबाधकपरमार्थज्ञानशुद्धचित्तोऽहम् ।
प्रकृतिरहं विकृतिरहं परिणतिरहमस्मि भागधेयानाम् ॥ १३१ ॥

para-jīva-bheda-bādhaka-paramārtha-jñāna-śuddha-
citto'ham
prakṛtir-ahaṁ vikṛtir-ahaṁ pariṇatir-aham-asmi
bhāgadheyānām

para-jiva-bheda **difference between the Supreme and the individual** badhaka **precluding** paramartha-jnana **the Knowledge of Reality/of the Supreme Truth** suddha-cittah-aham **I am one with a pure mind** prakrtih-aham **I am the natural/the original** vikrtih-aham **I am the modification** parinatih aham-asmi **I am the fulfillment** bhagadheyanam **of all that is fortunate**

I am one with a pure mind with the Knowledge of
Reality, the Supreme Truth,
That precludes the difference between the Supreme
and the individual.
I am the natural (original) and the modification.
I am the fulfillment of all that is fortunate.

132

फणधरभूधरवारणविग्रहविधृतप्रपञ्चसारोऽहम् ।
फालतलोदितलोचनपावकपरिभूतपञ्चबाणोऽहम् ॥१३२ ॥

phaṇa-dhara-bhū-dhara-vāraṇa-vigraha-vidhṛta-
prapañca-sāro'ham
phāla-talodita-locana-pāvaka-paribhūta-pañca-
bāṇo'ham

phana-dhara **the serpent** bhu-dhara **the mountain** varana **the elephant** vigraha **form** vidhrta **supporting** prapanca **the manifest world** sarah **the essence** aham **I am** phala-tala-udita **emanating from the forehead** locana **eye** pavaka **fire** paribhuta **humiliated** pancabanah **with five arrows (the god of love)** aham **I am**

I am the essence that supports the manifest world
In the form of the serpent, the mountain, and the elephant.
I am the one who humiliated the one with five arrows (the god of love)
By the fire emanating from the eye on the forehead.

133

बद्धो भवामि नाहं बन्धान्मुक्तस्तथापि नैवाहम् ।
बोध्यो भवामि नाहं बोधोऽहं नैव बोधको नाहम् ॥ १३३ ॥

baddho bhavāmi nāhaṁ bandhān-muktas-tathāpi naivāham
bodhyo bhavāmi nāhaṁ bodho'haṁ naiva bodhako nāham

baddhah **the bound** bhavami na-aham **I do not become/am not** bandhat **from bondage** muktah **liberated** tatha-api **that way also** na-eva-aham **I am not indeed** bodhyah **one who is to be taught** bhavami na-aham **I do not become** bodhah-aham na-eva **I am not the teaching either** bodhakah na-aham **I am not the one who is to teach**

I do not become the bound.
I am not the liberated from bondage either.
I do not become the one who is to be taught,
Nor am I the teaching, nor the one who is to teach.

134

भक्तिरहं भजनमहं भुक्तिरहं भुक्तिमुक्तिरहमेव ।
भूतानुशासनोऽहं भूतभवद्भव्यमूलभूतोऽहम् ॥१३४ ॥

bhaktir-ahaṁ bhajanam-ahaṁ bhuktir-ahaṁ bhukti-
muktir-aham-eva
bhūtānuśāsano'haṁ bhūta-bhavad-bhavya-mūla-
bhūto'ham

bhaktih-aham **I am devotion** bhajanam-aham **I am worship** bhuktih-aham **I am enjoyment** bhukti-muktih-aham-eva **I am also liberation from enjoyment** bhuta-anusasanah-aham **I am the ruler of beings** bhuta-bhavat-bhavya **the past, present, and future** mula-bhutah-aham **I am the one who is the origin**

I am devotion. I am worship.
I am enjoyment. I am also liberation from enjoyment.
I am the ruler of beings.
I am the one who is the origin of the past, present, and future.

135

मान्योऽहमस्मि महतां मन्दमतीनाममाननीयोऽहम् ।
मदरागमानमोहितमानसदुर्वासनादुरापोऽहम् ॥ १३५ ॥

mānyo'ham-asmi mahatāṁ manda-matīnām-
amānanīyo'ham
mada-rāga-māna-mohita-mānasa-durvāsanā-
durāpo'ham

manyah-aham-asmi **I am one to be revered** mahatam **of the great** manda-matinam **among the slow-witted** amananiyah-aham **I am not one to be regarded** mada **arrogance** raga **passion** mana **vanity** mohita **deluded** manasa-durvasana **evil vasanas of the mind** dur-apah-aham **I am difficult of reach**

I am one to be revered as among the great.
I am not one to be regarded as among the
slow-witted.
I am difficult of reach for the mind deluded
By evil tendencies like arrogance, passion,
and vanity.

136

यजनयजमानयाजकयागमयोऽहं यमादिरहितोऽहम् ।
यमवरुणयक्षवासवराक्षसमरुदीशवह्निरूपोऽहम् ॥ १३६ ॥

yajana-yajamāna-yājaka-yāga-mayo'haṁ yamādi-rahito'ham
yama-varuṇa-yakṣa-vāsava-rākṣasa-marud-īśa-vahni-rūpo'ham

yajana **the sacrificial rite** yajamana **the sacrifical host** yajaka **the sacrifical priest** yaga **the sacrifice** mayah-aham **I am of the nature of** yama-adi **restraint of senses and such** rahitah aham **I am devoid of** yama **Yama (god of death) (deity of south)** varuna **Varuna (deity of water) (deity of west)** yaksa **Yaksa (deity of wealth) (deity of north)** vasava **Indra (the ruler of the gods) (deity of east)** raksasa **Nirruti (the demon) (deity of southwest)** marut **Vayu (the deity of wind) (deity of northwest)** isa **Isana (Siva, the Lord) (deity of northeast)** vahni **Agni (deity of fire) (deity of southeast)** rupah-aham **I am of the nature of**

I am of the nature of the sacrificial rite, the sacrificial host,
The sacrificial priest, and the sacrifice.
I am devoid of restraint of the senses and such.
I am of the nature of Yama, Varuna, Yaksa, Indra, Nirruti, Vayu, Isa, and Agni.

137

रक्षाविधानशिक्षावीक्षितलीलावलोकमहिमाहम् ।
रजनीदिवसविरामस्फुरदनुभूतिप्रमाणसिद्धोऽहम् ॥ १३७ ॥

rakṣā-vidhāna-śikṣā-vīkṣita-līlāvaloka-mahimāham
rajanī-divasa-virāma-sphurad-anubhūti-pramāṇa-
siddho'ham

raksa-vidhana **affording protection** siksa-viksita **giving the sight of Knowledge** lilavaloka **[by] a playful look** mahima-aham **I am the glory** rajani-divasa-virama **night and day the cessation** sphurat **flashing in the mind** anubhuti **experience** pramana-siddhah-aham **I am one having the certitude of the authority**

I am the glory of the playful look
Affording protection and the vision of Knowledge.
I am one having the certitude of the authority
Of the flashing in the mind at the cessation of night
and day.

138

लक्षणलक्ष्यमयोऽहं लाक्षणिकोऽहं लयादिरहितोऽहम् ।
लाभालाभमयोऽहं लब्धव्यानामलभ्यमानोऽहम् ॥ १३८ ॥

lakṣaṇa-lakṣya-mayo'haṁ lākṣaṇiko'haṁ layādi-
rahito'ham
lābh-ālābha-mayo'haṁ labdhavyānām-
alabhyamāno'ham

laksana-laksya **the indicated and the denoted** mayah-aham **I am of the nature of** laksanikah-aham **I am the secondary sense (a word can have the indicated or obvious, the denoted or implied, and the secondary or derived sense)** laya-adi-rahitah-aham **I am devoid of dissolution and such** labha-alabha-mayah-aham **I am of the nature of gain and loss** labdhavyanam **of those to be attained** alabhyamanah-aham **I am one that cannot be attained**

I am of the nature of the indicated, denoted, and
derived sense.
I am devoid of dissolution and such.
I am of the nature of gain and loss.
Of those to be attained, I am one that cannot be
attained.

139

वर्णाश्रमरहितोऽहं वर्णमयोऽहं वरेण्यगण्योऽहम् ।
वाचामगोचरोऽहं वचसामर्थेन गम्यमानोऽहम् ॥ १३९ ॥

varṇāśrama-rahito'haṁ varṇa-mayo'haṁ vareṇya-
gaṇyo'ham
vācām-agocaro'haṁ vacasām-arthena
gamyamāno'ham

varnasrama-rahitah-aham **I am devoid of castes and prescribed orders of life** varna-mayah-aham **I am the alphabet (sacred syllables)** varenya-ganyah-aham **I am to be counted among the most excellent** vacam-agocarah-aham **I am beyond the range of speech** vacasam-arthena **by the meaning of words (of the aphorisms)** gamyamanah-aham **I am the one to be reached**

I am devoid of castes and prescribed orders of life.
I am the sacred syllables, and I am to be counted among the most excellent.
I am beyond the range of speech.
I am the one to be reached by the meaning of the words (of the aphorisms).

140

शमदमविरहितमनसां शास्त्रशतैरप्यगम्यमानोऽहम् ।

शरणमहमेव विदुषां शकलीकृतविविधसंशयगणोऽहम् ॥ १४० ॥

śama-dama-virahita-manasāṁ śāstra-śatair-apy-
agamyamāno'ham
śaraṇam-aham-eva viduṣāṁ śakalīkṛta-vividha-
saṁśaya-gaṇo'ham

sama **peace** dama **self-restraint/self-control** virahita-manasam **for minds devoid of** sastra-satair-api **even by hundreds of scriptures** agamyamanah-aham **I am not attainable** saranam-aham-eva **I only am the refuge** vidusam **of the realized ones** sakalikrta **shattered to pieces** vividha-samsaya **various doubts** ganah **multitude** aham **I am**

I am not attainable even by hundreds of scriptures
For minds devoid of peace and self-control.
I alone am the refuge of the realized ones.
I am one who has shattered to pieces the multitude of
various doubts.

141

षड्भावविरहितोऽहं षड्गुणरहितोऽहमहितरहितोऽहम् ।
षट्कोशविरहितोऽहं षट्त्रिंशत्तत्त्वजालरहितोऽहम् ॥ १४१ ॥

ṣaḍ-bhāva-virahito'haṁ ṣaḍ-guṇa-rahito'ham-ahita-rahito'ham
ṣaṭ-kośa-virahito'haṁ ṣaṭ-triṁśat-tattva-jāla-rahito'ham

sad-bhava-virahitah-aham **I am without the sextet of states** sad-guna-rahitah-aham **I am devoid of the sextet of qualities** ahita-rahitah-aham **I am devoid of anything not beneficial** sat-kosa-virahitah-aham **I am without the sextet of sheaths** sat-trimsat **thirty-six** tattva-jala **web of principles (factors of experience)** rahitah-aham **I am devoid of**

I am without the sextet of states, and I am devoid of the sextet of qualities.
I am devoid of anything not beneficial.
I am without the sextet of sheaths.
I am devoid of the web of thirty-six tattva-s.

142

संवित्सुखात्मकोऽहं समाधिसंकल्पकल्पवृक्षोऽहम् ।
संसारविरहितोऽहं साक्षात्कारोऽहमात्मविद्यायाः ॥ १४२ ॥

saṁvit-sukhātmako'haṁ samādhi-saṁkalpa-kalpa-
vṛkṣo'ham
saṁsāra-virahito'haṁ sākṣāt-kāro'ham-ātma-vidyāyāḥ

samvit-sukhatmakah-aham **I have in me the Bliss of Consciousness** samadhi-sankalpa **the sankalpa (determination) for samadhi (absorption in meditation)** kalpa-vrksah-aham **I am the celestial wish-fulfilling tree** samsara-virahitah-aham **I am without the samsara (birth-death cycle)** saksatkarah-aham **I am the direct Realization** atma-vidyayah **of Self-Knowledge**

I have in me the Bliss of Consciousness.
I am the celestial, wish-fulfilling tree for the
sankalpa (determination) for samadhi.
I am without the samsara.
I am the direct Realization of Self-Knowledge.

143

हव्यमहं कव्यमहं हेयोपादेयभावशून्योऽहम् ।
हरिरहमस्मि हरोऽहं विधिरहमेवास्मि कारणं तेषाम् ॥ १४३ ॥

havyam-ahaṁ kavyam-ahaṁ heyopādeya-bhāva-
śūnyo'ham
harir-aham-asmi haro'haṁ vidhir-aham-evāsmi
kāraṇaṁ teṣām

havyam-aham **I am the oblation to the gods** kavyam-aham **I am the oblation to the manes** heya-upadeya **rejection and acceptance** bhava-sunyah-aham **I am one without the attitudes** harih-aham-asmi **I am Hari (Visnu)** harah-aham **I am Hara (Siva)** vidhih-aham **I am the Creator (Brahma)** eva-asmi **I alone am** karanam tesam **the cause of these**

I am the oblation to the gods; I am the oblation
to the manes.
I am without the attitudes of rejection and
acceptance.
I am Hari; I am Hara; I am Brahma.
I alone am the cause of these.

144

क्षालितकलुषभयोऽहं क्षपितभवक्लेशजालहृदयोऽहम् ।
क्षान्ताद्यक्षरसुघटितविविधव्यवहारमूलमहमेव ॥ १४४ ॥

kṣālita-kaluṣa-bhayo'haṁ kṣapita-bhava-kleśa-jāla-
hṛdayo'ham
kṣāntādy-akṣara-sughaṭita-vividha-vyavahāra-mūlam-
aham-eva

ksalita-kalusa-bhayah **the fear of sin washed away** aham **I am** ksapita **thrown away, cast off** bhava-klesa-jala **the web of afflictions of samsara** hrdayah-aham **I am one with the heart** ksa-anta-adi-aksara **letters ending with ksa and others** sughatita **well-structured** vividha **various** vyavahara-mulam **root of interactions** aham-eva **I alone am**

I am one with the fear of sin washed away.
I am one with a heart from which the web of
afflictions of samsara has been cast off.
I alone am the root of various well-structured
interactions
Brought about by the letters ending with ksa and
such.

145

बहुभिः किमेभिरुक्तैरहमेवेदं चराचरं विश्वम् ।
शीकरफेनतरङ्गाः सिन्धोरपराणि न खलु वस्तूनि ॥ १४५ ॥

bahubhiḥ kim-ebhir-uktair-aham-evedaṁ carācaraṁ viśvam
śīkara-phena-taraṅgāḥ sindhor-aparāṇi na khalu vastūni

bahubhih kim **what avails so many** ebhih-uktaih **of these statements** aham-eva **I alone am** idam cara-acaram-visvam **this moving and unmoving universe** sikara **the spray** phena **the foam** tarangah **the waves** sindhoh **of the ocean** aparani **different** na khalu vastuni **things they are not**

What avails so many of these statements?
I alone am this moving and unmoving universe.
The spray, foam, and waves of the ocean
Are not, indeed, things different (therefrom).

146

शरणं न भवति जननी न पिता न सुता न सोदरा नान्ये
परमं शरणमिदं स्याच्चरणं मम मूर्ध्नि देशिकन्यस्तम् ॥ १४६ ॥

śaraṇaṁ na bhavati jananī na pitā na sutā na sodarā
nānye
paramaṁ śaraṇam-idaṁ syāc-caraṇaṁ mama mūrdhni
deśika-nyastam

saranam **refuge** na bhavati janani **is not the mother** na pita **nor father** na suta **nor sons** na sodara **nor brothers** na anye **nor others** paramam saranam **the supreme refuge** idam syat-caranam **is this foot** mama murdhni **on my head** desika-nyastam **placed by my Master**

The refuge is not the mother,
Father, sons, brothers or others;
The supreme refuge is this foot
Placed on my head by the Master.

147

आस्ते देशिकचरणं निरवधिरास्ते तदीक्षणे करुणा ।
आस्ते किमपि तदुक्तं किमतः परमस्ति जन्मसाफल्यम् ॥ १४७ ॥

āste deśika-caraṇaṁ niravadhir-āste tad-īkṣaṇe karuṇā
āste kimapi tad-uktaṁ kim-ataḥ param-asti janma-
sāphalyam

aste desika-caranam **when the Master's foot is there** niravadhih **limitless** aste tat-iksane **when there exists in his look** karuna **Grace** aste kim-api **when there exists anything at all** tat-uktam **said by him** kim-atah param-asti **what exists further** janma-saphalyam **the fruition of life**

When there exists the foot of the Master,
When there exists limitless Grace in his look,
When there exists anything at all of what he has said,
What further fruition of life exists?

148

कारुण्यसारसान्द्राः काङ्‌क्षितवरदानकल्पकविशेषाः ।
श्रीगुरुचरणकटाक्षाः शिशिराः शमयन्ति चित्तसंतापम् ॥ १४८ ॥

kāruṇya-sāra-sāndrāḥ kāṅkṣita-vara-dāna-kalpaka-
viśeṣāḥ
śrī-guru-caraṇa-kaṭākṣāḥ śiśirāḥ śamayanti citta-
saṁtāpam

karunya-sara-sandrah **abundant with the essence of compassion** kanksita-vara-dana **granting the desired boons** kalpaka-visesah **the special kalpaka (wish-fulfilling) trees** sri-guru-carana **of the feet of the revered Guru** kataksah **the glances** sisirah **cool** samayanti **assuage** citta-samtapam **the anguish of the mind**

Abundant with the essence of compassion,
Granting the desired boons, the special kalpaka trees
Of the feet of the revered Guru, with the cool
glances,
Assuage the anguish of the mind.

149

कबलितचञ्चलचेतोगुरुतरमण्डूकजातपरितोषा ।
शेते हृदयगुहायां चिरतरमेकैव चिन्मयी भुजगी ॥ १४९ ॥

kabalita-cañcala-ceto-gurutara-maṇḍūka-jāta-paritoṣā
śete hṛdaya-guhāyāṁ ciratarm-ekaiva cinmayī
bhujagī

kabalita **having swallowed** cancala-cetah **the wavering mind** gurutara-mandukah **the weighty frog** jata-paritosah **with contentment/possessing satisfaction** sete **sleeps** hrdaya-guhayam **in the cave of the heart** cirataram **for a very long time** eka-eva **alone, by itself** cinmayi bhujagi **the serpent of Consciousness**

Having swallowed the wavering mind, the weighty frog,
There sleeps with contentment, in the cave of the heart,
For an extremely long time, alone by itself,
The serpent of Consciousness.

150

मयि सुखबोधपयोधौ महति ब्रह्माण्डबुद्बुदसहस्रम् ।

मायामयेन मरुता भूत्वा भूत्वा मुहुस्तिरोधत्ते ॥ १५० ॥

mayi sukha-bodha-payodhau mahati brahmāṇḍa-bud-
buda-sahasram
māyā-mayena marutā bhūtvā bhūtvā muhus-tirodhatte

mayi **in me** sukha-bodha-payodhau **in the ocean of happiness/Bliss and Knowledge** mahati **vast** brahmanda **universe** bud-buda-sahasram **a thousand bubbles** maya-mayena **of the nature of maya (illusion)** maruta **by the wind** bhutva bhutva **forming and forming** muhuh **again and again** tirodhatte **disappear**

In me, the vast ocean of Bliss and Knowledge,
A thousand universe-bubbles
Form repeatedly by the wind, of the nature of maya (illusion),
And disappear, again and again.

151

गुरुकरुणयैव नावा प्राक्तनभाग्यानुकूलमारुतया ।
दुःसहदुःखतरङ्गैस्तुङ्गः संसारसागरस्तीर्णः ॥ १५१ ॥

guru-karuṇayaiva nāvā prāktana-bhāgyānukūla-
mārutayā
duḥsaha-duḥkha-taraṅgais-tuṅgaḥ saṁsāra-sāgaras-
tīrṇaḥ

guru-karunaya-eva **only by the compassion of the Guru** nava **by the ship** praktana-bhagya **good fortune of former times** anukula-marutaya **by the favourable wind** duh-saha **intolerable** duhkha **sorrow** tarangaih-tungaih **with lofty waves** samsara-sagarah **the ocean of samsara (illusory cycle of birth and death)** tirnah **has been crossed**

Only by the ship of compassion of the Guru,
By the favorable wind of the good fortune of
former times,
The ocean of samsara, with lofty waves,
Of intolerable sorrow, has been crossed.

152

सति तमसि मोहरूपे विश्वमपश्यं तदेतदित्यखिलम् ।
उदितवति बोधभानौ किमपि न पश्यामि किं न्विदं चित्रम् ॥ १५२ ॥

sati tamasi moharūpe viśvam-apaśyaṁ tad-etad-ity-akhilam
uditavati bodha-bhānau kimapi na paśyāmi kiṁ nvidaṁ citram

sati tamasi **when there was darkness** moha-rupe **of the nature of delusion** visvam **the universe** apasyam **I saw** tat-etat **that and this** iti **thus** akhilam **all** uditavati **when arose** bodha-bhanau **the sun of Knowledge** kim-api **anything at all** na pasyami **I do not perceive** kim nu-idam citram **what a wonder is this!**

When there prevailed the darkness of the nature of delusion,
All the universe I saw as "this" and "that;"
When the sun of Knowledge has arisen,
I do not perceive anything at all! What a wonder is this!

152
(alternate version)

नाहं नमामि देवान्देवानतीत्य न सेवते देवम् ।
न तदनु करोति विधानं तस्मै यतते नमो नमो मह्यम् ॥ १५२ ॥

nāhaṁ namāmi devān-devān-atītya na sevate devam
na tad-anu karoti vidhānaṁ tasmai yatate namo namo mahyam

Another version of the same verse:
nāhaṁ namāmi devān-devān-atītya na sevate devam
na tadanu karoti vidhānaṁ tasmai yatate namo namo mahyam

na aham namami **I do not salute** devan **the gods** devan atitya **transcending the gods** na sevate devam **one does not salute/serve a god** na tadanu **not thereafter** karoti **performs** vidhanam **scriptural injunctions** tasmai **therefore** yatate **endeavours** namah namah **prostrations again and again** mahyam **to Myself**

I do not salute the gods.
Transcending gods, one does not worship a god;
Nor, thereafter, does one endeavour to perform scriptural injunctions.
Prostrations again and again, to Myself!

153

इत्यात्मबोधलाभं मुहुरनुचिन्त्य प्रमोदमानेन ।
प्रारब्धकर्मणोऽन्ते परं पदं प्राप्यते हि कैवल्यम् ॥ १५३ ॥

ity-ātma-bodha-lābhaṁ muhur-anucintya pramoda-
mānena
prārabdha-karmaṇo'nte paraṁ padaṁ prāpyate hi
kaivalyam

Another version of the same verse:
ity-ātma-bodha-lābhaṁ muhur-apy-anucintya moda-
mānena
prārabdha-karmaṇo'nte paraṁ padaṁ prāpyate sma
kaivalyam

iti **thus** atma-bodha-labham **the gain of Self-Knowledge** muhuh **again and again** anucintya **thinking about, reflecting upon** pramodamanena **by him who rejoices** prarabdha-karmanah **of the prarabdha karma (past deeds that have come to fruition)** ante **at the end** param padam **the Supreme State** prapyate hi **is reached indeed** kaivalyam **the state of being That which alone is**

Thus, by him, rejoicing again and again,
Reflecting upon the gain of Self-Knowledge,
Finally, at the end of the fruition of past deeds,
The Supreme State is reached, indeed, the State of
being That which alone is (Kaivalyam).

154

मोहान्धकारहरणं संसारोद्वेलसागरोत्तरणम् ।
स्वात्मनिरूपणमेतत्प्रकरणमन्तर्विचिन्त्यतां सद्भिः ॥ १५४ ॥

mohāndhakāra-haraṇaṁ saṁsārodvela-sāgarottaraṇam
svātma-nirūpaṇam-etat-prakaraṇam-antar-vicintyatāṁ
sadbhiḥ

moha-andhakara-haranam **dispelling/destroying the darkness of delusion** samsara **samsara (birth-death cycle)** udvela-sagara-uttaranam **the crossing of the overflowing, shoreless ocean** sva-atma-nirupanam **definition of one's own Self** etat-prakaranam **this text** antah **inwardly** vicintyatam **let this be thought over** sadbhih **by the true**

Dispelling the darkness of delusion,
Carrying one across the overflowing ocean of
samsara (the birth-death cycle),
Let this text, the *Definition of One's Own Self,*
Be reflected upon inwardly by the true.

154
(alternate version)

मोहान्धकारहरणं संसारोद्वेलसागरोत्तरणम् ।

स्वात्मनिरूपणमेतत् प्रकरणमकुरुत दक्षिणामूर्तिः ॥ १५४ ॥

mohāndhakāra-haraṇaṁ saṁsārodvela-sāgarottaraṇam
svātma-nirūpaṇam-etat prakaraṇam-akuruta
dakṣiṇāmūrtiḥ

moha-andhakara-haranam **dispelling the darkness of delusion** samsara **samsara (the birth-death cycle)** udvela-sagara-uttaranam **crossing the overflowing, shoreless ocean** svatmanirupanam **definition of one's own Self** etat prakaranam **this text** akuruta **composed** daksinamurtih **Daksinamurti**

Dispelling the darkness of delusion,
Carrying one across the overflowing, shoreless ocean
of the samsara,
This text, the *Definition of One's Own Self,*
Was composed by Daksinamurti (Dakshinamurti).

155

अज्ञानान्ध्यविहन्ता विरचितविज्ञानपङ्कजोल्लासः ।

मानसगगनतलं मे भासयति श्रीनिवासगुरुभानुः ॥ १५५ ॥

ajñān-āndhya-vihantā viracita-vijñāna-paṅkajollāsaḥ
mānasa-gagana-talaṁ me bhāsayati śrīnivāsa-guru-
bhānuḥ

ajnana-andhya **blinding ignorance** vihanta **which destroys** viracita **blossoming** vijnana-pankaja **the lotus of Knowledge** ullasah **joy** manasa **mind** gagana-talam **sky** me **mine** bhasayati **illumines** srinivasa-gurubhanuh **the sun that is the Guru, Srinivasa (the abode of Sri, Lord Visnu, the abode of fortune and radiance)**

Destroying the blinding ignorance
And giving the joy of the blossoming lotus of
Knowledge,
The sky of my mind
Is illumined by the sun that is the Guru, who is
Srinivasa (Lord Visnu).

श्रीमत्परमहंसपरिव्राजकाचार्यस्य
श्रीगोविन्दभगवत्पूज्यपादशिष्यस्य
श्रीमच्छंकरभगवतः कृतौ
स्वात्मनिरूपणं संपूर्णम् ॥

śrīmat-paramahaṁsa-parivrājakācāryasya
śrī-govinda-bhagavat-pūjya-pāda-śiṣyasya
śrīmac-chaṁkara-bhagavataḥ kṛtau
svātmanirūpaṇaṁ saṁpūrṇam

Of the venerable, glorious, highest renunciate,
wandering recluse and great spiritual teacher,
Sri Govinda Bhagavan, whose feet are to be
worshipped,
The disciple, the venerable, glorious Sankara
Bhagavan, [by him] composed,
Definition of One's Own Self concludes.

For further instruction in Nondual Truth, Self-Knowledge, and Self-inquiry, or for a list of other SAT publications, please contact:

Society of Abidance in Truth (SAT)
1834 Ocean Street, Santa Cruz, California 95060 USA
Ph: (831) 425-7287
Email: sat@satramana.org
Web: www.SATRamana.org

If you are interested in helping to support the publication of this book and similar spiritual books, you are warmly invited to contact us.